MICROSCOPIC
LIFE

Previous page: An SEM of *Dendrocometes paradoxus*,
a ciliate protist around 100μm long that lives on the gills
of *Gammurus*, a small crustacean. Its branching "tentacles"
catch passing food particles. Magnification: **x1,600**

This page: This LM shows two species of the dinoflagellate
Ceratium, a plantlike protist. *Ceratium* is found in plankton,
the tiny mass of microscopic organisms that float on the
surface water of oceans. Magnification: **x370**

KFK KINGFISHER KNOWLEDGE

MICROSCOPIC LIFE

Richard Walker

Foreword by
Professor Peter C. Doherty

KINGFISHER

BOSTON

Senior editor: Carron Brown
Coordinating editor: Stephanie Pliakas
Senior designer: Peter Clayman
Picture researcher: Rachael Swann
Consultant: Dr. John Grainger, Chairman of MISAC
  (Microbiology in Schools Advisory Committee)
Production controller: Lindsey Scott
DTP coordinators: Sarah Pfitzner, Jonathan Pledge
DTP operator: Primrose Burton
Artwork archivists: Wendy Allison, Jenny Lord
Proofreaders: Sheila Clewley, Sarah Snavely

KINGFISHER
a Houghton Mifflin Company imprint
222 Berkeley Street
Boston, Massachusetts 02116
www.houghtonmifflinbooks.com

First published in 2004
10 9 8 7 6 5 4 3 2 1
B&N/0605/EURO/MA(MA)/130MA/C

LIBRARY OF CONGRESS CATALOGING-IN-PUBLICATION DATA
Walker, Richard, 1951-
Microscopic life/Richard Walker.—1st ed.
p. cm.—(Kingfisher knowledge)
Includes index.
1. Microbiology—Juvenile literature. I. Title. II. Series.
QR57.W34 2004
579—dc22
2004001321
ISBN 0-7534-5778-4

Printed in Italy

Contents

GO FURTHER . . .
INFORMATION PANEL KEY:

web sites and further reading

career paths

places to visit

NOTE TO READERS (1)
The web site addresses listed in this book are correct at the time of going to print. However, due to the ever-changing nature of the Internet, web site addresses and content can change. Web sites can contain links that are unsuitable for children. The publisher cannot be held responsible for changes in web site addresses or content or for information obtained through third-party web sites. We strongly advise that Internet searches should be supervised by an adult.

NOTE TO READERS (2)
All measurements are abbreviated throughout this book. Please see pages 10–11 for an explanation of the measurements and their abbreviations.

SEM of *Trichinella* roundworms
Magnification: x660

Foreword

My life as a research scientist has been spent trying to understand how the body deals with the invasion of simpler life-forms such as bacteria, fungi, and viruses. We know what we can see. Before the microscope and before the germ theory of disease, people thought that infections were a property of "miasmas" (toxic vapors), of malevolent acts by evil enemies, or resulted from the whim of the gods. In the plague years of the Middle Ages minorities were killed for "poisoning the wells," and isolated women were burned at the stake for practicing witchcraft.

With Antoni van Leeuwenhoek, for the first time humans saw the minutiae of life that surrounds us. Microscopy opened up the study of bacteriology. Robert Koch could stain and see the *tubercle* bacillus (the bacterium that causes tuberculosis) through the lens of his microscope. I recently purchased an elegant, brass instrument built in 1882 by the firm of Ernst Leitz in Wetzlar, Germany. The year 1882 came after Darwin's publication *On the Origin of Species* but before Ronald Ross discovered the *plasmodium* protozoan that causes malaria. My antique Leitz monocular would have no trouble showing the malaria parasite. It could not, however, be used to see the influenza viruses or the human immunodeficiency virus (HIV), which is the focus of my current research program. Such organisms can be visualized only using the electron microscopes that, with the progress of technology, continue to advance our understanding.

My contemporary, 21st-century research group uses a diverse range of sophisticated instrumentation to analyze the characteristics of the virus-specific host response. This equipment ranges from flow cytometers that depend on laser and computer technology to characterize and separate the responding lymphocyte populations to thermal cyclers that amplify molecular messages for analysis using genome technology. We use instruments that combine light microscopy and digital technology to measure the magnitude of cellular immunity. Most of our experiments begin with a young scientist or technician examining the cell populations with a conventional light microscope that is not very different from my 1882 veteran.

Modern science—and the progressive revolution it has brought to the human condition—has been in progress for around 500 years. Van Leeuwenhoek, whose simple microscopes can be seen today in the Boerhaave Museum in Leiden, Netherlands, lived from 1632–1723. The first of the great scientific academies, the Royal Society of London and the science section of the Académie Française, were founded in 1660 and 1663 respectively. The microscope has been with us from the earliest days of this enormous enterprise that has so illuminated the natural world for us and so changed the way that we live and think. The capacity to see is there for those who choose to look and learn.

Professor Peter C. Doherty—joint winner of the 1996 Nobel Prize for Physiology or Medicine and fellow of the Royal Society in the United Kingdom

CHAPTER 1

Micro life revealed

Imagine an object as small as the sharp point of a needle—something so small we can barely see it. Now try to imagine something even smaller. Beyond our vision exists an amazing world populated by huge numbers of tiny creatures called microorganisms (or microbes), hundreds or thousands of times smaller than that needle tip. We know these creatures exist because microscopes magnify the tiniest life-forms to make visible what was previously invisible. The study of microorganisms is called microbiology. As well as microorganisms, such as viruses and bacteria, microscopes also allow us to see fungal spores, mini animals, and plant pollen in detail. For 150 years microbiologists have studied microbes to understand what they look like and how they live. Because of them, micro life has been revealed.

Unseen world

The world around us is teeming with tiny living things. Some are barely visible to the naked eye, but many are so small they can be seen only with a microscope. These tiny living things include mini animals and smaller life-forms called microorganisms or microbes. There is an amazing variety of microbes, and they are found almost everywhere on Earth. On these pages you can see four creatures that live unseen in the microscopic world. Their size on the page is no guide to their size in real life—the mini animal *Daphnia* is 150 times bigger than the microbe *Chlamydomonas*!

A world of variety

Inhabitants of the microworld include viruses, bacteria, protists, microscopic fungi, and mini animals. Chemical packages called viruses are the smallest microbes of all. Bacteria, such as *Streptococcus*, consist of single, simple cells. Protists consist of single cells and include algae such as *Chlamydomonas*. Fungi are mostly multicellular and can be large, such as mushrooms, or microscopic such as the soil fungus *Arthrobotrys*. Mini animals are multicellular and include minute crustaceans such as *Daphnia*.

▶ This SEM shows *Streptococcus* bacteria taken from a person with a throat infection. The spherical-shaped bacteria, each between 0.7 and 1 μm long, are often linked together in a chain.

▲ A microbiology researcher investigates cells infected with a virus. The whole procedure takes place inside a special cabinet with a screen separating the researcher from the cells. He is wearing a face mask, gloves, and protective clothing in order to reduce the possibility of being infected by the virus.

Lifestyles

Microorganisms lead many different lifestyles. Protists include those, like animals, that take in food and those, like plants, that make food by photosynthesis. Some fungi are parasites, but many also gain nutrients from dead plants and animals. Bacteria include *Streptococcus*, a pathogen (disease-causing microbe) that can live in humans and make us sick. But only one in 10,000 types of bacteria causes disease. Others live harmlessly on living things, and many more feed on dead or decaying material. All viruses are parasites, and most cause diseases because they invade living cells (of bacteria, animals, or plants) in order to reproduce.

Magnification: **x52,940**

▶ A deadly underground ambush is taking place in this SEM, where the hyphae (threadlike parts) of the soil fungus *Arthrobotrys* ensnare and digest a roundworm.

Magnification: **x400**

Magnification: **x130**

◀ A crustacean that is 1.5mm long, water flea *Daphnia* lives in ponds and feeds by filtering tinier organisms out of its surroundings.

Habitats

Microorganisms are everywhere. A microscopic snapshot of the back of your hand—or anywhere else on your skin— would reveal billions of bacteria. Look at soil, rocks, clouds, lakes, oceans, deserts, or mountaintops, and bacteria will be there, too. Other microbes are also widespread. Protists live in puddles, ponds, tree trunks, and seas, not to mention blood vessels and intestines. Tiny fungal spores float through the air and grow wherever the right food is found. And there are so many tiny soil roundworms that if all of Earth's soil was blown away, the shape of the continents would be preserved by the roundworms' bodies!

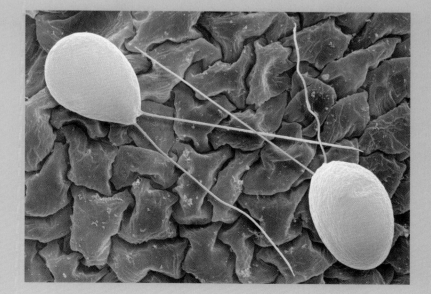

▲ This SEM shows two pear-shaped green algae called *Chlamydomonas*, which live in freshwater and move rapidly by beating the two whiplash flagella on their front ends. Each is around 10μm long (not including flagella). *Chlamydomonas* uses sunlight energy to make its own food. Magnification: **x2,950**

Size and scale

Because they cannot be seen with the naked eye, it can be difficult to understand how small microbes really are or how small the smallest is compared to the biggest. This is made more confusing because micrographs enlarge microscopic organisms by different amounts, so the tiniest can look bigger than the largest. In this book measurement and magnification are clearly shown, as explained below.

▶ A dust mite (see page 31) rests on the tip of a sewing needle. Magnification makes it look 130mm long. In reality it is only 0.3mm long. The magnified mite is 130 ÷ 0.3 = 433 times larger than life size.

100nm (0.1μm or 0.0001mm)

▲ VIRUS—Magnification: **x500,000**
Viruses are the smallest microbes, and most are between 10 and 100nm in size. This flu virus (see page 22) is 85nm across.

1μm (0.001mm)

▲ BACTERIUM—Magnification: **x50,000**
This sore-throat-causing *Streptococcus* bacterium (see pages 8–9) is around 1μm long. Most bacteria are between 1 and 4μm long.

10μm (0.01mm)

▲ PROTIST—Magnification: **x5,000**
This trypanosome protist (see pages 48–49) is around 10μm long, ten times bigger than *Streptococcus*. Most protists are 10 to 200μm long.

Measuring microorganisms

Throughout this book the size of microorganisms is given in metric units, the system of measurement used by all scientists around the world. Measurement of length (see table on the opposite page) is based on the meter (m), although this is too big to be useful here. Few of the organisms in the book are longer than one millimeter (mm)—one thousand times smaller than one meter and the width of the letter "i" in the word "Size" in the heading at the top of this page. Most microbes are much smaller and are measured in micrometers (μm), or thousandths of one millimeter. Viruses are even smaller and are measured in nanometers (nm), or millionths of one millimeter.

Scale and magnification

All of the microorganisms in this book are shown larger-than-life. We use scale and magnification to understand how an organism's size on a page relates to its real size. The six squares above show how this works. In the first square (top left) 50mm (the width of the square) represents 100nm (0.0001mm) in real size. That is a scale of 50:0.0001 or 500,000:1. So the virus in the square has been magnified, or enlarged, 500,000 times (x500,000). In the second square 50mm represents 1μm, a scale of 50,000:1, magnifying the bacterium 50,000 times. So in real life the bacterium is around ten times bigger than the virus. Similarly, the next square represents an organism ten times bigger, and so on.

Magnification: **x433**

100μm (0.1mm)

▲ FUNGUS—Magnification: **x500**
Fungi range in size from tiny yeast cells to large puffballs. Each fungal filament, or hypha (see page 9), is 10μm across.

1mm (0.1cm)

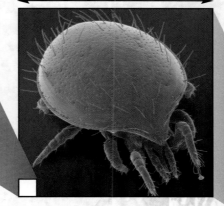

▲ MINI ANIMAL—Magnification: **x50**
This eight-legged mite (see page 15) is 1mm long, making it barely visible to the naked eye. Many other mini animals are smaller, even as small as 100μm.

10mm (1cm)

▲ HOVERFLY—Magnification: **x5**
Around 10mm long, this garden hoverfly is easily seen. Included here only for comparison, it is 100,000 times bigger than the flu virus.

1 meter (m)	= 100 centimeters or 1,000 millimeters
1 centimeter (cm)	= 10 millimeters
1 millimeter (mm)	= 1,000 micrometers (μm)
1 micrometer (μm)	= 1,000 nanometers (nm)

single lens

object placed
on a pin

◀ Van Leeuwenhoek's microscope
consisted of a single convex lens
clamped between two brass plates.
It was held as shown, and the
flat side was brought up close
to the eye. The specimen, placed
on a pin, was then viewed through
the lens held against a source
of light such as a candle.

Under the microscope

At the end of the 1500s a remarkable invention changed the study of organisms forever. Hans and Zacharias Janssen, a father-and-son team of eyeglass makers in the Netherlands, constructed an instrument (later called the compound microscope) that used two glass lenses to magnify tiny objects. In the 1600s Antoni van Leeuwenhoek and Robert Hooke used microscopes to reveal a world previously hidden from human sight. That world is populated by tiny organisms that are less than 0.2mm (200μm) across, too small to be seen with the naked eye.

Van Leeuwenhoek's animalcules

Dutch cloth merchant Antoni van Leeuwenhoek (1632–1723) made his own simple microscope using only one small convex lens that could magnify up to 300 times. By examining samples taken from soil, puddles, and other sources, he became the first person ever to see microorganisms, which he called "animalcules," or "tiny animals." Van Leeuwenhoek made detailed drawings and between 1674–1676 established his reputation by reporting his findings to the Royal Society of London in England. In 1683 he saw numerous tiny organisms in scrapings taken from his teeth, the first time that bacteria had ever been seen. As van Leeuwenhoek noted: "There are more animalcules in the scum on the teeth in a man's mouth than there are men in a whole kingdom."

Hooke's discoveries

English scientist Robert Hooke (1635–1703) built his own compound microscope, which could achieve magnifications of x300 and x500, although the images were blurred at the edges. Despite this, Hooke used his excellent drawing skills to record his findings in the book *Micrographia*, published by the Royal Society in 1665. One drawing showed a thin slice of cork containing many tiny "chambers." Hooke called them "cells," the word we now use to describe the building blocks of life (see pages 18–19).

Compound microscopes

Compound microscopes today are also called light microscopes because they use light to illuminate organisms. Light passing though a specimen is magnified by the microscope's objective (lower) lens and then again by the eyepiece (upper) lens before being seen as an enlarged image. Light microscopes usually magnify up to x1,000. A photograph taken using a light microscope is called a light micrograph (LM).

◀ This drawing of a cross section through cork, taken from Robert Hooke's *Micrographia*, shows the tiny chambers he called "cells."

Contrast and staining

Most microorganisms are transparent, and so they are invisible to us even when magnified. Contrast makes an organism or its parts visible by making it stand out from its surroundings. An easy way to do this is to use chemicals called stains that add color to organisms, as shown in the picture below. However, most stains can be used only when organisms are dead, and so they cannot be seen moving. One way to see living organisms is to use different forms of lighting to obtain contrast such as showing the specimen as a bright object on a dark background (see the LM of *Vorticella* on page 18).

▲ This LM shows a blood smear taken from a person with the disease sleeping sickness. A blue stain has been added to reveal trypanosomes, the protists that cause the disease, among the circular red blood cells. Magnification: **x1,000**

◀ A scientist uses a modern compound microscope to examine a specimen. The three objective lenses provide increasing powers of magnification.

Smaller and smaller

Invented in the 1930s, powerful electron microscopes can magnify tiny objects much more than any light microscope can. Electron microscopes have transformed our understanding of microscopic life by allowing scientists to explore the structure of tiny organisms in great detail and to see very small objects, such as viruses, for the first time. The four micrographs shown here were produced using either transmission or scanning electron microscopes. In each case false colors have been added to the otherwise black-and-white image.

Transmission electron microscopes

Imagine sitting in the dark and shining a flashlight through your fingers. When the flashlight beam hits your hand, the light is scattered by your fingers, and the shadow image of your hand is projected onto a wall. Transmission electron microscopes work in a similar way but use tiny particles called electrons instead of light. An electron "gun" at the top of the tubelike microscope fires a fast-moving beam of electrons through a thin slice of the specimen. Some parts of the specimen scatter electrons, just like your fingers scatter the flashlight beam. The beam of scattered electrons is then focused by magnets onto a TV screen to reveal a magnified view of the specimen. This image can be "captured" as a transmission electron micrograph (TEM).

► This TEM shows a section through a bacterium called *Bordetella pertussis*. Around 1.4µm long, it causes the disease whooping cough, or pertussis. Magnification: **x58,825**

◄ A cross section of the virus that causes hepatitis, a liver disease, is shown in this TEM. Each virus particle (a blue circle) is only 30nm wide. Magnification: **x392,000**

▲ This SEM shows the external features of a 1mm-long mite (a relative of spiders) that lives in dead leaves and decaying wood. Magnification: **x70**

Zooming in on the surface

Scanning electron microscopes are used to examine whole (not sectioned) organisms. When a narrow beam of electrons scans a specimen, electrons bounce off of the organism's surface and are picked up by a detector that produces an image on a TV screen. The image is a highly detailed 3-D view of the specimen's surface. While light microscopes can magnify up to 1,000 times (x1,000) and resolve (distinguish between) two objects $0.2\mu m$ apart, a scanning electron microscope can magnify up to x10,000 and resolve objects 20nm apart. A transmission electron microscope can magnify more than x300,000 and resolve objects less than 1nm apart.

Magnification:
x880

▲ Around 0.3mm across, this is the outer skeleton of a radiolarian, a type of protist that floats in the surface waters of warm seas. The SEM shows the tiny holes through which the single-celled organism pushes out microscopic threads to collect food.

▶ Each on-screen image shows a 3-D image of an ant's head produced using the scanning electron microscope at the back of the picture. A beam of electrons speeds down the tube part of the microscope, bounces off the object (an ant), and forms an image. The researcher (left) uses a computer link to move the ant around so she can see different views of its body, as well as to increase or decrease the magnification in order to show more or less detail. The view on screen can be "captured" at any time as an SEM.

Life from nowhere?

From the time of the ancient Greeks, around 2,400 years ago, until the 1800s there was a widespread belief that living organisms could arise from nonliving or decaying matter. This sudden appearance of life from nowhere was called spontaneous generation. The discovery of microorganisms in the 1600s made spontaneous generation seem even more possible. It took the work of a brilliant French scientist to finally disprove the idea.

Spontaneous generation

Greek philosopher Aristotle (384–322 B.C.) thought the idea that small animals, such as worms, arose spontaneously from mud was simply common sense. This belief was passed down over the centuries. Almost 2,000 years after Aristotle's death Belgian scientist Jan Baptista van Helmont (1579–1644) left wheat grains wrapped in sweaty shirts inside an open barrel. When, after 21 days, mice were found there, van Helmont concluded that they had arisen spontaneously from the sweat and wheat. He had "proved" that spontaneous generation existed!

Maggots from meat

Another common belief was that maggots arose spontaneously from rotting meat. In 1668 Italian doctor Francesco Redi (1626–1697) tested this idea. He placed meat in two containers—one open to the air and one covered with gauze that allowed air into the container but not flies. The meat in the open container was soon covered with maggots. The covered meat remained maggot free because flies could not reach the meat to lay their eggs. Redi's experiment disproved the spontaneous generation of maggots.

▲ Maggots (fly larvae) feeding on meat do not arise spontaneously.
They hatch from eggs laid by female flies. Magnification: **x3**

▼ Held up by Louis Pasteur, a flask with a snapped-off neck contains cloudy, contaminated broth. In the unbroken swan-necked flask, in front of him, the broth remains clear and sterile.

▶ Far from arising spontaneously, bacteria are descendants of ancient life-forms. More than two billion years old, these cyanobacteria-containing stromatolites in Australia are the oldest structures made by living things.

Pasteur's proof

Despite Redi's work, people still believed that microbes could arise spontaneously. But in 1859 microbiologist Louis Pasteur (1822–1895) settled the matter. He placed clear broth in a flask and heated the flask's neck in order to shape it into a curve shaped like a swan's neck. He then boiled the broth to sterilize it (make it microbe free). Once cool, it stayed sterile and clear even though it was exposed to the air—any microbes from the air had been trapped in the curved neck. When he snapped off the neck, microbes got into the broth and made it cloudy as they multiplied. Pasteur had proved that life arises only from preexisting life.

▲ An artist's view inside the alga *Chlamydomonas* shows that it contains a chloroplast (green) as well as standard cell components. It moves using two whiplike flagella. Magnification: **x5,500**

The building blocks of life

Every organism on Earth, from the smallest bacterium to the mightiest whale, is made up of tiny living units called cells. Some organisms, such as protists, consist of only one cell. Others are made up of thousands, millions, or even billions of cells. Using microscopes, scientists have shown that while the cells of protists, fungi, plants, and animals—known as eukaryotic cells—vary in shape and size, they share many common features. Bacterial cells, known as prokaryotic cells, also share some of these features but have a simpler structure (see pages 24–25).

Inside a eukaryotic cell

Before the invention of the electron microscope cells were known to have only an outer boundary (plasma membrane) surrounding a control center (nucleus) and, between them, a jellylike cytoplasm. Powerful electron microscopes then showed that the cytoplasm is more than a simple liquid and that it also contains tiny structures called organelles ("little organs"), such as mitochondria (singular—mitochondrion), that release energy from sugars by a process called cell respiration. This process powers all the chemical reactions that take place inside the cell that make it stay alive. The folded membranes of the endoplasmic reticulum transport cell-building proteins made by the specklike ribosomes. The nucleus holds DNA—the genetic material that contains the instructions needed to construct and operate the cell.

▶ This cross section through a "typical" animal cell shows features that are found in all eukaryotic cells.

◀ This LM shows *Vorticella*, a protozoan (animallike) protist that consists of a bell-shaped "head" and a long stalk attached to a water plant or a stone. The "head" carries hairlike cilia that beat in order to draw in food. One *Vorticella*, around 0.3mm long, is extended and feeding, and the other is contracted. Magnification: **x480**

Single cells

Most eukaryotic, unicellular (single-celled) microorganisms belong to the protists, the group that includes algae and protozoa. Algae, such as *Chlamydomonas*, make their food by photosynthesis. In addition to standard eukaryotic cell parts, *Chlamydomonas* has a green chloroplast packed with light-trapping chlorophyll. Protozoa, such as *Vorticella*, either capture food or absorb it from their surroundings. Fixed in place, *Vorticella* has hairlike cilia that beat to create a current to draw in food. Its more mobile relatives use cilia to move. Other protozoa have long flagella that push or pull them through water. Other unicellular microbes include yeasts—microscopic fungi that absorb food from their surroundings.

cytoplasm

nucleus

endoplasmic reticulum

ribosomes

mitochondrion

plasma membrane

▲ This LM shows *Caenorhabditis elegans*, a 1mm-long roundworm that lives in soil. *C. elegans* is a mini animal and is multicellular, but unlike most animals, it consists of a fixed number of cells (959).
Magnification: **x180**

▲ This LM shows that human cheek cells have a nucleus (orange) and a cytoplasm (green).
Magnification: **x825**

▶ This 50μm-long human sperm (pink) is about to fertilize a much larger, spherical egg, or ovum, (orange) in this illustration. Its flagellum (tail) beats in order to move the sperm.
Magnification: **x2,800**

Many cells

Many multicellular organisms, such as plants, some fungi, and many animals are too big to be featured in this book. However, their cells can only be seen using a microscope—such as the sidewalklike cells that line the inside of our cheeks. Also, in order to reproduce, humans and other organisms release microscopic sex cells, such as sperm and eggs, that fuse to produce a new organism. Note that the sperm (right) has a flagellum like those of *Chlamydomonas* (opposite, top left). Mini animals, such as roundworms and mites, are also multicellular, although they consist of fewer cells. For example, *Caenorhabditis elegans*, a roundworm, has 959 cells, while a human adult has around 100 trillion.

SUMMARY OF CHAPTER 1: MICRO LIFE REVEALED

An SEM of *Phthiracarus*— a soil mite that lives unseen in leaf litter. A relative of spiders, this mini animal also has eight legs. It helps recycle nutrients by feeding on dead plant material.
Magnification: x75

Introducing the microworld

Unseen but all around us is a hidden world of microscopic organisms. They range in size and variety from millionths-of-a-millimeter-long viruses to bacteria, protists, and microscopic fungi to mini animals, such as water fleas, that are barely visible to the naked eye. We can easily understand the difference in size between a mouse and an elephant. But the "invisibility" of micro life makes it difficult for us to comprehend how small they are or even how a water flea, for example, is 15,000 times bigger than a virus.

In this chapter we have seen how the millimeter (mm), micrometer (μm), and nanometer (nm) are used to measure and show differences in size between microbes. We have also learned how magnification makes a microscopic organism appear bigger so that, for example, being magnified 100 times (x100) means that the object is 100 times bigger than in real life.

Making things bigger

Invented only 400 years ago, microscopes changed our view of life by bringing the microworld into view for the first time. The first microscopes used light to illuminate minute specimens, and their more sophisticated descendants are still used today. But more powerful electron microscopes, invented in the 1900s, allow us to look deeper into the microworld by magnifying microscopic organisms much more and by allowing us to see tiny creatures in much greater detail. Microscopes (both light and electron) have also enabled scientists to find out how cells—the basic units of all life, including microorganisms—are built, how they function, and how they always arise from other cells.

Go further . . .

 Visit an interactive web site about microbes at:
www.amnh.org/nationalcenter/infection

Find more about microbes at:
www.microbeworld.org

Compare the sizes of microbes at:
www.cellsalive.com/howbig.htm

For more information about Robert Hooke and Antoni van Leeuwenhoek, visit:
www.ucmp.berkeley.edu/history/hooke.html *and*
www.ucmp.berkeley.edu/history/leeuwenhoek.html

See some amazing micrographs at:
www.denniskunkel.com/

 Biochemist
Studies the chemical reactions that take place inside cells, including those of microorganisms.

Cell biologist
Studies cells, their structure, and how they work.

Microbiologist
Biologist who specializes in the study of microorganisms, especially bacteria and viruses.

Microscopist
Using light and/or electron microscopes, examines and photographs cells and microorganisms.

 See some of Antoni van Leeuwenhoek's microscopes at:
Museum Boerhaave
Lange Sint Agnietenstraat 10
2313 WC, Leiden, Netherlands
Phone: +31 71 5214224
www.museumboerhaave.nl

Visit the "Tools of Science" exhibit at the Museum of Science and Industry in Chicago to explore the use of computer-based imaging technology:
Museum of Science and Industry
57th Street and Lake Shore Drive
Chicago, IL 60637
Phone: (773) 684-1414
www.msichicago.org

CHAPTER 2

Microscopic organisms

There are trillions and trillions of microscopic organisms—so many that despite each microbe being so small, together they far outweigh the planet's bigger life-forms by more than ten times. Even more astoundingly, they are found everywhere, from high up in the atmosphere to the dark depths of the ocean, not to mention inside our noses, on our food, and lurking in our beds. To make sense of this teeming mass of microscopic creatures, we classify, or group, them into groups according to their shape, structure, size, lifestyle, and how they are related to each other. These groups are viruses, bacteria, protists, fungi, and mini animals.

This SEM shows *Hydra,* a freshwater mini animal, anchored by its base to some pondweed. Its pink color is completely artificial. It has been added to an otherwise black-and-white micrograph in order to provide contrast so that the *Hydra's* parts can be seen clearly.
Magnification: x100

Magnification:
x675,000

virus envelope
with protein
spikes

protein coat
(capsid)

nucleic acid
(RNA)

Viruses

Of all microbes, viruses are the smallest and strangest. These nonliving chemical packages don't feed or grow, and they become active only when they invade living cells, called hosts, in order to reproduce. Many viruses cause diseases in animals and plants. Viruses range in size from 25 to 300nm.

▲ This computer illustration shows the structure of a flu (influenza) virus, 85nm across. It has an outer protein coat, studded with spikes, and a core of nucleic acid (in this case RNA).

Chemical packages

Every virus is made up of a handful of chemical components. The core is made of a strand or strands of nucleic acid—either DNA or RNA—that carry the instructions to make more viruses. Surrounding this core is a protective protein coat called a capsid. This has spikes that enable the virus to attach itself to the surface of a host cell. Capsids vary greatly in shape. Some have regular shapes with straight sides, while others are less regular. Viruses can invade all types of cells, including those of animals, plants, fungi, protists, and bacteria. Bacteria-invading viruses are called bacteriophages. Unable to move on their own, viruses can be transferred from host to host in droplets in the air, in water or food, in infected blood, or by bloodsucking or plant-biting insects.

▼ A T4 bacteriophage virus (red), 250nm in height, injects its DNA through the cell wall of an *Escherichia coli* bacterium in this TEM. This virus has a complex shape with a regular "head," a "tail," and six "legs."

Magnification:
x350,000

▼ This SEM shows an aphid using its piercing mouthparts to penetrate leaf cells in order to feed on sugary sap. These insects carry viruses and spread them between plants while feeding.
Magnification: **x65**

► This diagram shows how a virus reproduces, using a bacteriophage and its *E. coli* host as an example:
1) Virus attaches to the bacterium
2) Virus tail injects DNA into bacterium
3) Virus DNA and proteins made inside bacterium
4) Newly assembled viruses emerge from bacterium

1

2

▶ This computer-generated image shows SARS (Severe Acute Respiratory Syndrome) viruses traveling through the air in water droplets as they pass from an infected person to be breathed in by an uninfected person. Clearly visible are the capsid (green) and its spikes (red). First identified in 2003, the virus causes a severe and sometimes fatal disease. It belongs to the coronaviruses, the group that usually causes mild or moderate respiratory (breathing) infections, such as colds, in humans. Magnification: **x600,000**

Virus reproduction

All viruses share the same life cycle, one that is completely different from any living organism. The illustration (below left) shows the reproduction of a bacteriophage, but the same principles apply to other viruses. First the virus locks onto its target cell and then penetrates the cell and releases its DNA or RNA load. Once the DNA or RNA instructions have penetrated the host cell, they hijack its chemical machinery so that it begins to produce multiple copies of the virus' nucleic acid core and protein coat. Once these components are made, they are assembled into new virus particles. No longer required, the host cell bursts open to release the virus copies that then go on to infect other cells and copy themselves once again.

Changing identity

Our body's immune system usually remembers a virus' identity so it does not infect us again. But some viruses, such as the flu virus, can change their identity and infect us repeatedly. In addition, altering its identity can allow a virus to "jump" from animals to humans. This is what happened in 2003 when the SARS disease appeared in Asia. The virus, normally found in catlike civets, had changed and was able to infect human cells. Spread by coughs and sneezes, the new disease caused severe breathing problems. Around 8,000 cases and 750 deaths occurred worldwide as SARS spread out of Asia before it was brought under control.

▼ A Chinese woman wears a face mask to help protect her from being infected with SARS. The SARS virus, like common cold viruses, is carried through the air in tiny water droplets. The mask absorbs droplets and stops the woman from breathing in virus particles.

3

4

Bacteria

The smallest and most abundant of all living things, bacteria are everywhere—on land, in water, in the air, even on and in other living things. Each bacterium consists of a single, simple cell, and most live in groups or colonies within which they usually reproduce rapidly. Bacteria are often feared for the diseases they cause such as food poisoning. But many bacteria benefit us by helping produce the conditions that enable life on Earth to exist.

capsule

cell wall

▲ Bacteria not only live in clouds (background), but they also grow and multiply there, as Austrian scientists discovered in 2000. Incredibly these bacteria, which originate from plants or soil on Earth's surface, may also influence climate by affecting cloud formation and rainfall.

Bacterial cells

Bacteria are prokaryotic cells, simpler in structure than the complex eukaryotic cells (see pages 18–19). Like eukaryotic cells, bacteria have a cytoplasm, a plasma membrane, and ribosomes that make the cell's proteins, but they lack a nucleus. Instead they have a nucleoid, a single loop of DNA containing the instructions needed to make and run the cell. Bacteria hold their shape with a rigid cell wall, and some have a slimy outer jacket (the capsule) that protects them. Short "hairs" called pili attach the bacteria to their food, and many also have longer flagella that beat and move them.

◄ This SEM compares the shapes of the three main types of bacteria. These are spherical bacteria, or cocci (purple); rod-shaped bacteria, or bacilli (pink); and spiral-shaped bacteria (blue). Magnification: **x10,000**

Sizes and shapes

Most bacteria are between 1μm and 4μm long—only visible in detail using an electron microscope. Around 10,000 species of bacteria are known, although there are certainly many, many more. They can be divided into three groups—cocci, bacilli, and spiral bacteria—according to their shape. Cocci (singular—coccus) are round and can occur singly, in pairs, in clumps, or in chains, as in *Streptococcus* (see page 8). Bacilli (singular—bacillus) are straight, rod-shaped bacteria that include *Escherichia coli*. Spiral-shaped bacteria include corkscrewlike forms called spirochetes and comma-shaped cells called vibrios.

▲ 0 minutes—
1 bacterium

▲ 20 minutes—2 bacteria

◄ Starting with a single bacterium, this LM sequence shows the rapid multiplication of *E. coli*, a normally harmless bacillus that lives in our large intestines. Grown on a nutrient agar gel at 77°F (25°C), the bacteria divide by binary fission every 20 minutes. Magnification: **x1,000**

▲ 1 hour and 40 minutes—
32 bacteria

nucleoid

cytoplasm

pili

plasma
membrane

▲ 3 hours—
512 bacteria

▼ 4 hours—
4,096 bacteria
(not all shown)

flagella

▲ This cutaway view of a bacillus around 4μm long shows the main features of most bacterial cells, including its cell wall and capsule. Magnification: **x55,000**

ribosomes

Locations and lifestyles

Bacteria live everywhere—in the air, soil, oceans, and even the cleanest bathrooms. Most bacteria absorb food from their surroundings, including dead matter, such as fallen leaves or raw meat, or living things such as human skin or cow's stomachs. Some use sunlight energy and photosynthesis to make their food. Bacteria reproduce by copying their DNA and then dividing into two identical cells—a process called binary fission. Given warmth and plenty of food, bacteria can divide every 20 minutes. This means that, in theory, one bacterium could give rise to five billion trillion (5,000,000,000,000,000,000,000) bacteria in only 24 hours!

Protists

Found mostly in oceans and freshwater, as well as damp places on land, protists are single-celled organisms that show an incredible variety of forms, including sunlike heliozoans, sculptured diatoms, and amoebas that constantly change shape. Protist cells are eukaryotic and have their DNA enclosed inside a nucleus. Protists are usually divided into two main groups—protozoa and algae.

Protozoa
Protozoa track down and gather food in the form of bacteria, other protists, or particles of dead matter. They can be grouped as flagellates, amoeboids, or ciliates, according to how they move. Flagellates have one or two long, whiplike flagella that beat to pull or push them through water. Amoeboids change shape, pushing out temporary pseudopodia ("false feet") to pull themselves along a solid surface. Some amoeboids have shells with holes through which they stick out their pseudopodia, while others, such as amoebas, are "naked." Ciliates have many small, hairlike projections called cilia that beat rhythmically, enabling them to move, turn, or stop rapidly.

Magnification: x875

◄ This SEM shows *Euglena*, a green freshwater flagellate found in ponds and puddles that usually makes its own food by photosynthesis. The long flagellum at its front end pulls *Euglena* through the water.

Algae
These plantlike protists use sunlight energy and photosynthesis to make their food. Algae include green algae, diatoms, dinoflagellates, and euglenas. Many live on the surface waters of oceans and lakes where sunlight can penetrate, with some moving along with the water and others by using their flagella. Together, this mass of floating algae forms phytoplankton (see pages 54–55), vitally important because of the life-giving oxygen it releases. Algae are also found in soil and on rocks and tree trunks, as well as in the green slime in ponds and puddles. Some algae, such as *Euglena*, can also feed on other protists.

Protozoan lifestyles

The dramatic image below shows the predatory ciliate *Didinium* about to engulf its prey. Like many protozoa, once the prey is "swallowed," it is enclosed inside the cell in a "bag" called a food vacuole and is then digested. This is true of most protozoa that live freely in seas, lakes, ponds, and in the soil. But a few protozoa are parasites that absorb food directly from their hosts (see pages 48–49). These parasites include the pathogenic protists that cause sleeping sickness, malaria, and, in the case of *Entamoeba*, dysentery. Whether they are parasites or free living, most protozoa reproduce by dividing in two (binary fission).

Magnification: **x3,230**

▶ This SEM shows *Entamoeba*, a pathogenic amoeba, around 35µm long, with pseudopodia. It is about to divide into two.

absorption

digestion

food vacuole

food particle

waste

▶ This sequence shows how an amoeba takes in food, forms a food vacuole, digests the food, absorbs nutrients, and then gets rid of waste.

◀ Barrel-shaped predator *Didinium* attacks fellow ciliate *Paramecium* in this SEM. *Didinium* fires a paralyzing poison dart into the 150µm-long *Paramecium* and then opens its "snout" to swallow its much larger prey. Both move using their cilia, arranged in two "belts" in *Didinium* and as a complete covering in *Paramecium*.

Magnification: **x2,130**

▶ Heliozoans, or "sun animals," are freshwater and marine amoeboids that resemble a shining sun. Freshwater *Actinophrys*, seen in this LM, has a "body" that is 50µm across and uses its needlelike pseudopodia, called axopodia, to move and to capture food. Magnification: **x120**

Fungi

Neither a plant nor an animal, fungi form a group of living things that includes mushrooms, toadstools, and puffballs, as well as mildew on plants, mold on bread, and yeasts. But if almost all of these fungi can be seen without a microscope, why should they be included in this book? There are three reasons. Firstly because although large fungi look smooth, they are actually made up of a mass of microscopic threads. Secondly because of they way they feed and, finally, because of the tiny spores they release in order to reproduce.

Feeding threads

Fungi do not make food using sunlight, as plants and algae do, nor do they roam in search of food and then eat it, as many animals do. Instead fungi feed through microscopic threads called hyphae that grow through a food source. The network of fungal hyphae—called a mycelium—releases enzymes, which are chemicals that digest or break down the chosen food into a "soup" of simple nutrients that are absorbed into the hyphae. The mycelium of a bread mold (below) spreads through bread, while that of a mushroom can extend through the soil of an entire field. Most fungi, such as mushrooms and molds, are saprobes— they feed on dead animal and plant material. But some are parasites, feeding on living organisms and causing diseases such as athlete's foot in humans and mildew in plants.

▶ Like most fungi, this puffball, *Lycoperdon pyriforme*, reproduces by forming spores that are spread through the air. As can be seen here, puffballs force out clouds of millions of microscopic spores through an opening in the top of their fruiting bodies.

◀ This slice of bread is almost unrecognizable because it is covered in a layer of woolly bread mold. Tangled hyphae can be seen here growing up from the bread, at the top of which are black, spherical fruiting bodies. These burst open to release tiny spores.
Magnification: **x12**

Magnification:
x3,800

▲ These grapes are covered in a grayish waxy layer made by millions of yeast cells that feed on sugary juices that ooze out through the grapes' skins.

◄ This SEM shows yeast cells, with the largest being around 10μm across.

"parent" cell

"daughter" cell budding

Single cells

Not all fungi are made of hyphae. Yeasts are microscopic fungi that exist as individual single cells. They reproduce by a process called budding. A "parent" yeast cell produces a new cell, or bud (above left), which remains attached to the parent and then separates to lead its own life. Yeast cells absorb nutrients directly from their surroundings. Those living on fruits, for example, obtain energy from the fruits' sugar-rich juices and release carbon dioxide. This process is used in bread making (see page 38). Some yeasts are parasites such as the one that causes the disease thrush in humans.

Billions of spores

The hyphae of most fungi grow invisibly through food sources including bread, soil, wallpaper paste, floorboards, bird droppings, fallen leaves, fruits, or living animal and plant tissues. But in order to reproduce, fungi form visible fruiting bodies that release microscopic spores into the air. In microscopic molds these fruiting bodies are spheres that cover woolly growths of hyphae and burst in order to release their contents. In larger forms a tightly packed mycelium of hyphae forms a puffball (left) from which billions of spores can be released in a short time. In every case the minute spores, each containing one or two fungal cells, float in the air. Those that land on a suitable food source will germinate there and grow into a new fungus.

Mini animals

Mention the word "animal" to someone, and they will probably think of something easily visible such as a lion or a bee. But there are many microscopic animals—let's call them mini animals—that live unnoticed by us. They include *Hydra* (a relative of sea anemones), minute crustaceans (relatives of crabs and lobsters), tiny mites, pseudoscorpions (the cousins of spiders), and mini insects, as well as many other types of animals. Like their larger relatives, mini animals are made up of many cells and live by taking in food, either from plants or other animals—or both. Mini animals are found everywhere, but on these pages we focus on three habitats—soil, water, and our homes.

**Magnification:
x17.5**

▲ Less than 3mm long, pseudoscorpions live in leaf litter. Like scorpions, their larger, distant relatives, they have claws, but they lack the scorpion's curved tail and stinger.

In the soil

Soil and leaf litter (rotting leaf and plant material in the soil) are swarming with mini animals. Along with soil fungi and bacteria, primitive insects, such as springtails and proturans, feed on dead animals and plants. A handful of soil contains millions of microscopic worms called roundworms, which have smooth, cylindrical bodies. They feed on rotting material, as well as fungi and plant roots. There are also hunters in the soil. Pseudoscorpions ("false scorpions") track down prey by touch and then use their pincers to grab and inject poison into their prey before sucking out the juices from the paralyzed victims.

bud

Magnification: **x140**

circle of cilia

stomach

toe

◀ Around 0.5mm long, rotifers, or wheel animals, live in freshwater ponds. This one is attached to a plant by its "toe." The rotifer's head has two circles of hairlike cilia that beat like revolving wheels, making currents that draw food particles into its mouth and stomach. Magnification: **x150**

In the water

A whole new world of animal life is revealed by putting a drop of pond water under a microscope. Close to the surface are zooplankton (also see pages 54–55), tiny animals that feed on tinier animals or plants and, in turn, provide food for larger animals. Some are larvae that will grow into bigger adults. Others, including *Cyclops*—which finds its food (algae and dead animals) by touch—spend their lives there. Some other pond animals, such as rotifers and *Hydra*, live attached to plants or stones. *Hydra* grabs passing prey using its armed tentacles. It reproduces by growing a bud that eventually drops off to form a new individual.

▲ Named after the one-eyed giant from Greek mythology, single-eyed *Cyclops*, a tiny crustacean around 2mm long, flicks its long, feathery antennae in order to pull it through the water of ponds and lakes. This female *Cyclops* is easily identified by two full egg sacs that contain her unborn young. Magnification: **x24**

▼ This SEM shows a pond-dwelling *Hydra*, around 1.5mm long, with its bud (offspring). Attached firmly to a plant, *Hydra* fires paralyzing threads into passing prey, which is pulled into the mouth by its tentacles.

mouth

At home

In even the cleanest home tiny creatures lurk unseen. The most numerous of these, with more than 5,000 in one gram of dust, are dust mites. Found wherever there is a plentiful supply of skin flakes, such as mattresses, dust mites squirt their digestive juices onto dead skin and then suck up the tasty fluid that is produced. If dust containing mite droppings is breathed in, it can cause asthma in some people. Other tiny home dwellers include book lice and fleas, both wingless insects. Only 2mm long, book lice feed on the pages of old books, leaving tiny holes as evidence of their presence. Dark brown and the size of a pinhead, fleas feed on the blood of cats and other pets but will switch, reluctantly, to humans if they are hungry.

▼ A tiny relative of spiders, only 0.2mm long, this dust mite moves through the hairs and fibers that make up part of house dust in search of its favorite food—human skin flakes.

tentacle

Magnification: **x500**

SUMMARY OF CHAPTER 2: MICROSCOPIC ORGANISMS

TEM of a *Streptococcus* bacterium attached to a tonsil cell (blue) in the throat
Magnification: **x33,000**

Micro variety

The microscopic world is filled with variety. The microscopic organisms that inhabit it are mostly unicellular (consisting of a single cell), but there are also multicellular (many celled) species. To make sense of this mass of microlife we put it into categories based on the way these organisms look and live.

Packages, prokaryotes, and protists

Viruses, the simplest of all microbes, are chemical packages surrounded by a protective coat. They barely qualify as life-forms because they don't feed or move, and they can only reproduce by infecting a living cell. Each virus package is a set of instructions that creates more viruses—these instructions are set into motion when the virus infects a living cell. Bacteria, the most numerous and widespread organisms on Earth, consist of a single, prokaryotic cell—a specific bacterial cell that has no nucleus, unlike cells of other organisms. Protists—the plantlike algae and animallike protozoa—are bigger than bacteria and live in water and damp places.

Small and large

Two other groups of living things—fungi and animals—include some species that are microscopic (yeasts and rotifers) and others that are big (puffballs and elephants). Microscopic fungi, along with viruses, bacteria, and protists, are grouped together as microorganisms and studied by microbiologists. Fungi feed using tiny threads called hyphae that grow through a food source. In this book microscopic animals are called mini animals. Mini animals feed by taking in food just like their larger relatives do.

Go further . . .

 Visit the "smallest" page on the web to examine the bacteria, protists, and mini animals in a drop of water: www.microscopy-uk.org.uk/mag/wimsmall/smal1.html

The National Geographic "Bacteria Rule" web site gives information about bugs and germs at: http://nationalgeographic.com/world/0010/bacteria

For a clear description of microbes go to: www.microbe.org/microbes/what_is.asp *and* www.microbe.org

Microscopic Life by Theresa Greenaway (St. Martin's Press, 2002)

 Bacteriologist
Microbiologist who specializes in the study of bacteria.

Mycologist
Explores the biology and uses of molds, yeasts, and other fungi.

Parasitologist
Studies the structure, biochemistry, and life cycles of parasites.

Protozoologist
Studies animallike protists (protozoa).

Virologist
Microbiologist who studies viruses, the diseases they cause, and how they infect cells.

 The "Traits of Life" exhibition at the Exploratorium in San Francisco covers many microscopic life-forms:
The Palace of Fine Arts
3601 Lyon Street
San Francisco, CA 94123
Phone: (415) 561-0308
www.exploratorium.edu

See the "Hidden Kingdoms—The World of Microbes" exhibition at:
New York Hall of Science
47–01 111th Street
Queens, NY 11368
Phone: (718) 699-0005
www.nyhallsci.org

CHAPTER 3

Inside the microworld

A look inside the microworld reveals a lot about how microbes live and work. In fact, the more we discover about these tiny organisms, the more we realize how much they affect not only our lives but those of all living things on Earth. As Louis Pasteur wrote in 1869, "The role of the infinitely small is infinitely large." While it is true that throughout history microorganisms have had a negative impact on humans and other organisms by causing diseases, today we recognize how much many microbes help us and our fellow organisms. Put simply, without the microworld, life could not exist.

A colony of the mold *Penicillium notatum* grows on a nutrient medium. The discovery in 1928 by Alexander Fleming that a substance released by this fungus killed bacteria eventually led to the production of penicillin—the first antibiotic. Magnification: x4

Virus alert

Viruses are parasitic packages of chemicals that have to take over the cells of living organisms in order to reproduce themselves. Many cause diseases ranging from mild to very serious. We depend on our built-in immune, or defense, system to destroy invading viruses before they destroy us. Today we can be protected from known viral diseases, such as measles or rubella, by vaccinations, which "boost" our immune system. But viruses change, and we need to always be alert for newer, deadlier versions.

▲ A virus has given yellow streaks to this normally all-red tulip flower. Viral infections pass from one generation to the next and are prized by gardeners because of the colorful patterns they make.

Causing diseases

Virus infections can have harmless results such as altering a flower's color. But generally viruses cause diseases when they multiply and burst out from infected cells. Mild infections, such as colds, are easily wiped out. Others, such as mumps and measles, are normally overpowered by the immune system. But viruses can change their "identity," producing new, more dangerous strains that the immune system cannot identify. In 1918–1919 a new flu strain caused a worldwide epidemic that killed more than 20 million people—many more deaths than occurred during World War I (1914–1918).

◀ Researchers wear protective clothing as they study tissues from an African monkey that is suspected of carrying Ebola fever, a very unpleasant viral disease that is usually fatal in humans.

Magnification: x194,000

◀ ▲ A young boy (left) shows a blotchy measles rash. The measles virus (above, outlined in purple) is surrounded by a capsule made of human cell membranes, which help "hide" it from the body's immune system.

Tropical diseases

Yellow fever is a tropical disease, sometimes fatal, that gets its name from the yellowing of the skin that results from the virus damaging a person's liver. In the 1800s yellow fever was a serious problem in Central America. Its cause remained unknown until 1900, when U.S. Army doctor Walter Reed (1851–1902) and his team, working in Cuba, showed that yellow fever is caused by a virus and spread by mosquitoes. Today people can be protected against yellow fever by getting a vaccination, but the same is not true for some of the viral hemorrhagic (bleeding) fevers. In central Africa, for example, outbreaks of Ebola fever occur when the virus spreads from monkeys to humans or from humans to humans. The disease causes extensive internal bleeding and usually results in death.

▶ A female *Aedes aegypti* mosquito pushes her needlelike mouthparts through skin to feed on blood. Each time they feed, these mosquitoes may pass on one of two different tropical viral diseases—flulike dengue or more deadly yellow fever—picked up from another person's blood.

Magnification: x8

Destroying defenses

Some viruses target the immune system. They include HIV (Human Immunodeficiency Virus), identified in 1983, which causes AIDS (Acquired Immune Deficiency Syndrome). Important to our immune system are lymphocytes—cells that identify and destroy germs. HIV invades and multiplies inside the lymphocytes. This weakens a person's immune system, and eventually they develop AIDS—a condition in which the body is unable to fight off even common diseases. The body is overwhelmed by infections, and the person dies. There is no cure for AIDS at present, but certain drugs can slow down the progress of HIV.

▶ Seen in detail, 100nm across, HIV has "spikes" (yellow) that attach to lymphocytes.

▼ This SEM shows a human lymphocyte (green) infected with HIV, with new viruses (red) emerging from its surface.

Magnification: x520,000

Magnification: x7,300

Bacteria—enemies or friends?

Bacteria affect our lives in many ways. Some are harmful and make us sick. But others release life-giving oxygen into the air or recycle dead organisms in order to maintain a balance of nutrients in the air and soil. Other bacteria are used to make foods, such as cheese, as well as medicine and other useful chemicals. Without bacteria, plants, humans, and other animals would not exist.

Harmful bacteria

Some types of bacteria live on or in living things. Many are harmless and even help us, but others, known as pathogens (or germs), can cause diseases in animals and plants if they get inside of their tissues. In humans pathogenic bacteria cause serious diseases, including typhoid fever, tuberculosis (TB), plague, and meningitis, as well as milder conditions such as acne and tooth decay. Pathogenic bacteria usually harm an organism by releasing poisonous chemicals called toxins, which may disrupt cell activities or even destroy cells. Botulinum toxin, released by *Clostridium botulinum*, causes serious food poisoning called botulism in humans. It is the deadliest natural poison known—one drop could kill 100,000 people.

◄ ▼ The tooth below has a coating of plaque (yellow)—sticky food remains and masses of bacteria (SEM, left). If plaque is not removed by regular toothbrushing, bacteria feed on sugars, releasing acids that eat away tooth enamel and cause decay.

Magnification:
x3,880

Magnification:
x135

▼ In this photo taken during World War II (1939–1945) American soldiers are spraying mattresses in army barracks with an insect killer to destroy body lice. When the lice feed on human blood, they can spread a deadly bacterial disease called typhus.

▶ This TEM shows a cross section through a marine cyanobacterium called *Dermocarpa*. Clearly visible inside the bacterial cell, which is around 4 µm across, are membranes that contain the green pigment chlorophyll. Also found in plants, chlorophyll "traps" sunlight energy to make sugar (food) for the bacterium and also releases oxygen.
Magnification: **x17,350**

Part of nature

Most bacteria form part of the natural life of soil, water, and other habitats. Many release nutrients, such as carbon and nitrogen, that are needed by plants and animals. One group, the cyanobacteria, make food by trapping sunlight energy. This process, called photosynthesis, takes in carbon dioxide and releases oxygen. Ancestors of cyanobacteria first perfected photosynthesis more than two billion years ago, long before plants appeared. By 700 million years ago they had released enough oxygen into the atmosphere to allow the appearance of oxygen-breathing organisms and, eventually, humans.

Helping humans

We use bacteria for a wide range of purposes. Some bacteria produce antibiotics (used to kill pathogenic bacteria) and other medicine. Brewing, leather making, and other industries rely on chemicals produced by bacteria. Bacteria in the water at sewage treatment plants help break down human waste into harmless substances. Even the deadly botulinum toxin has a use—some people pay doctors to have it injected in a diluted form under the skin on their face to relax muscles and remove wrinkles.

▼ *Lactobacillus* and other bacteria play an important role in making cheese, yogurt, and other dairy products.

Fungi at work

Carried by the air, microscopic fungal spores grow into new fungi when they land on their preferred source of food. There they get to work, using threads called hyphae that penetrate and digest dead or living organisms and then soak up the nutrients that are released. By working this way, fungi affect humans in many ways, some helpful and some harmful. We use fungi as food and to make medicine. Fungi play a part in natural cycles of life, making dead things rot and releasing essential nutrients for new generations—but this rotting ability also damages our everyday materials. Fungi can make us sick and can cause disease in other animals and plants.

▲ Bread dough is left to rise in a warm place before being baked in the oven. Dough contains yeast, a single-celled fungus. Yeast breaks down sugar in order to obtain energy, releasing carbon dioxide gas, which makes the dough rise and gives bread its sponginess.

Helpful fungi

Microscopic yeasts feed on sugars to release both carbon dioxide gas—used to make bread rise—and ethanol (alcohol)—used to make drinks such as beer and wine. Mushrooms and their relatives are eaten in all types of foods. Molds, such as *Penicillium*, give Roquefort and other blue cheeses their blue streaks and Camembert and Brie their distinctive tastes. Fungi are also used to make soy sauce and to turn soybeans into the vegetable protein tofu. We use fungi to make bacteria-killing antibiotic drugs such as penicillin and other drugs, including cyclosporine, which is used to stop a body from rejecting transplanted organs such as kidneys.

▼ ▶ The fungal disease athlete's foot (below) produces itchy, sore, and cracked skin on the toes. The SEM (right) shows branching hyphae (orange) of *Trichophyton mentagrophytes*, one of the fungi that causes athlete's foot, spreading among skin flakes. The fungus feeds on keratin, a tough protein found in skin flakes and in the skin's outer layer, the epidermis. Athlete's foot can be treated using antifungal creams.

Magnification: **x4,350**

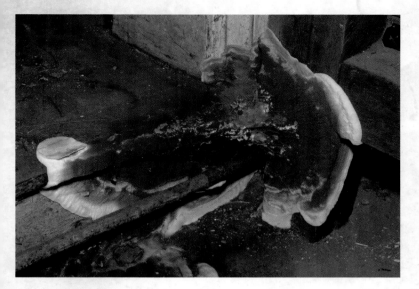

▲ This piece of timber is badly affected by *Serpula lacrymans*, a fungus that causes dry rot. Its thick bundles of hyphae spread over long distances, feeding on damp timber until the wood eventually crumbles. The only solution is to cut out rotting timber and then spray the area to prevent further attacks.

Decomposers

In forests, fields, and other habitats fungi play a vital role by helping break down, or decompose, dead plant and animal remains. These decomposers release important nutrients that plants and animals need in order to grow and thrive. But decomposing fungi make no distinction between a rotting tree in a forest and the floorboards in our houses. The dry rot fungus, for example, grows rapidly in damp conditions and quickly destroys floors unless it is treated. Other types of fungi rot fresh fruits, meat, bread, vegetables, and other foods, making them moldy and inedible. These food feeders include a fungus that attacks stored cereals and peanuts and then releases a poison called aflatoxin that kills thousands of people every year. Fungi can also attack and ruin most of the materials we use in everyday life, including paper, clothing, leather, paint, gasoline, and film.

Causing diseases

Pathogenic fungi are those that cause diseases by feeding on living, not dead, plants and animals. More than 5,000 types of fungi, including rust, smut, and mildew, attack economically important food crops, such as wheat and corn, making them inedible or poisonous. Fungi also infect, damage, and kill trees and garden plants such as roses. Other pathogenic fungi cause diseases in humans and other animals. Ringworm is caused by a ring-shaped, itchy fungal growth on the skin of the body or head. Thrush, or candidiasis, is caused by a white growth of a yeast in body openings such as the mouth.

▶ The brown, dusty marks seen in this close-up view of an ear of wheat are caused by *Puccinia graminis*, one of the "rust" fungi. Rust causes great damage to crops, such as wheat, and can result in heavy losses for farmers.

Infection and defense

People fight a constant battle to avoid invasion by a hostile army of pathogens, or germs. These are the microorganisms that cause infectious diseases. Once a pathogen gets inside the body, it causes an infection by growing rapidly and multiplying, which disrupts how the body works. An infected person shows symptoms and signs that are typical of the pathogen and the disease it causes. To prevent invasion by pathogens, the body has a series of barriers that form its outer defenses. Pathogens that manage to get through these barriers are usually then destroyed by the body's inner defenses.

Routes of infection

Pathogens arrive on or in the body by different routes, often from another person who is infected. Many diseases, such as chicken pox and colds, are spread when a person breathes in pathogens contained in droplets released from another infected person by a sneeze or cough. Some diseases, such as cold sores, are spread by direct touch between people. A few, including malaria, are spread by biting insects as they move from person to person, feeding on blood. Finally some diseases, such as food poisoning, are caused by eating food or drinking water that has been contaminated by pathogens from human and farm animal feces.

Outer defenses

To cause infections, a pathogen first has to break through the body's outer defenses. Skin is a watertight, germ-proof barrier that protects the body's insides. Sweat, tears, and saliva (spit) all contain antiseptic (germ-killing) chemicals. The nose and mouth are lined with tightly packed cells, like cobblestones, that stop pathogens from penetrating to the tissues below. The windpipe is coated with sticky mucus that traps airborne pathogens, which are then carried up to the throat and swallowed. In the stomach these pathogens are destroyed by powerfully acidic stomach juices.

▼ The tiny droplets forced out by this sneeze may contain coronaviruses (right, orange), each only 100nm across, which cause the common cold. If breathed in by another person, the viruses invade cells inside the nose and throat, causing a stuffy, runny nose and sore throat.
Magnification: x235,300

Magnification:
x1,175

◄ A common cause of food poisoning is the bacterium *Salmonella enteriditis*, shown in this TEM. Each around 1.25µm long, *Salmonella* bacteria enter the body on or in contaminated food, especially meat, chicken, eggs, and dairy products. In the small intestine *Salmonella* releases toxins that cause vomiting, pain, and diarrhea. Magnification: **x35,000**

▲ A kissing bug (*Rhodnius prolixus*) deposits feces on the skin as it feeds on human blood. The feces may contain a protist that causes Chagas' disease (which affects the heart and nervous system) when scratched into wounds made by the bug. Magnification: **x2.5**

Magnification: **x1,900**

▲ In this SEM a macrophage (orange), one of the body's phagocyte defenders, surrounds and destroys an invading protist called *Leishmania* (green). This pathogen, spread by tropical biting sand flies, causes skin ulcers on the site of the bite.

Inner defenses

The few pathogens that get past the outer barriers face the body's two inner defense mechanisms. Firstly, cells called phagocytes roam around the body in search of foreign invaders. Once found, they engulf the pathogens and digest them. Secondly, cells called lymphocytes form the body's immune system. These cells "remember" the identity of invading pathogens so that if they return, the lymphocytes release killer chemicals called antibodies that target and destroy each germ. Normally these inner defenses make sure that an infection is short-lived. But some infections need outside help in the form of drugs, such as antibiotics, in order to destroy the marauding pathogens.

◄ This SEM shows a needle tip covered by rod-shaped bacteria (orange), each around 4µm long. If this needle was used for an injection, it would pierce the skin, introduce bacteria into the body, and cause an infection. That is why it is important for doctors and nurses to use sterile (germ-free) needles.

Great epidemics

An epidemic happens when an infectious disease spreads rapidly and affects large numbers of people. For example, influenza (flu) epidemics happen every few years, and many people, especially in cities, get sick. Most people recover, but this was not the case in the great epidemics of the past. Smallpox, plague, cholera, measles, and tuberculosis (TB) were just some of the diseases that killed millions of people. But until the 1800s and 1900s no one understood the causes of these diseases—let alone how to treat them.

▶ Only 0.2μm across, a variola virus, the cause of smallpox, is shown in this computer-generated image. Like many other viruses, variola has an outer protein coat and a central core of DNA. Although smallpox has been destroyed, the variola virus is still used for scientific research.

Magnification:
x547,000

▼ Taken in 1973, this photo shows a young Bangladeshi child with smallpox. The spots and blisters that are typical of smallpox can be seen on his face and legs. Only seven years later, in 1980, the World Health Organization declared that smallpox had been wiped out.

The scourge of smallpox

Known since the earliest times, smallpox was a major killer. Caused by the variola virus, smallpox spread easily from person to person. An infected person had a fever and then got a rash that developed into pus-filled blisters that often scarred those who survived. Particularly at risk were those people who had no natural immunity. When, for example, the Spanish conquistadores arrived in Central America in 1519, they brought smallpox with them. Epidemics spread through the defenseless Native Americans, reducing their population from 30 million to three million in only 50 years. In the 1700s vaccinations were first used to prevent smallpox, and in the late 1970s the disease was finally eliminated.

▼ This 17th-century doctor wears a beaked mask. The beak was filled with strong-smelling herbs that covered up the smell of dead and decaying bodies. Also, not knowing how plague spread from person to person, some doctors believed that the strong herbal aromas could protect them from infections.

▲ This woodcut of the Great Plague of 1665 shows the dead being buried outside the walls of the city of London.

Death by plague

Plague is caused by a bacterium called *Yersinia pestis*. It is mainly a disease that affects rats, spread from rat to rat by the fleas that feed on their blood. But when rats die of the disease, the infected fleas feed on people and then spread the disease to them. These facts were unknown when an outbreak of plague, called the Black Death, spread from Asia and killed one third of Europe's population in the late 1340s. Victims developed large dark swellings, or buboes, and most died painful deaths soon afterward. Another plague epidemic in London, England, in 1665 killed up to 100,000 people. Today plague is rare and can usually be treated with bacteria-killing drugs.

◄ This painting shows Dr. Edward Jenner carrying out his first vaccination against smallpox in 1796.

Giving protection

Smallpox was a deadly disease with no cure. But Edward Jenner (1749–1823), an English doctor, noticed that milkmaids who caught the related but less harmful disease cowpox from their cows never caught smallpox. This gave him an idea. In 1796 he infected eight-year-old James Phipps with cowpox by scraping pus from a cowpox blister onto his arm. Six weeks later Jenner infected the boy with smallpox, but James did not develop this disease. His immune system had been triggered by cowpox to form a defensive shield against smallpox. In this way James Phipps experienced the first vaccination.

▼ Scottish bacteriologist Alexander Fleming in his London laboratory in 1943. He holds a petri dish containing *Penicillium* mold.

Microbe fighters

Although Antoni van Leeuwenhoek had seen and described bacteria as far back as 1683, by the mid-1800s doctors and scientists had not made the link between microbes and disease. Most believed that diseases were caused and spread by poisonous air that arose from stagnant ponds and human waste. Then a series of discoveries revealed not only that many diseases were caused by bacteria and viruses but also showed how to fight and destroy these microbes. We begin in the 1700s . . .

Germ theory

Vaccination protected James, but nobody knew why. Neither, in 1846, did Austrian doctor Ignaz Semmelweis (1818–1865) understand why insisting that his fellow doctors washed their blood- and pus-covered hands before treating patients greatly reduced death rates from infections. Other doctors even made fun of Semmelweis for suggesting that infections could be carried on their hands! Eventually answers were provided by French microbiologist Louis Pasteur (1822–1895) and German doctor Robert Koch (1843–1910) from the 1860s onward. Their germ theory proved once and for all that specific bacteria and, later, certain viruses cause specific diseases. Semmelweis was finally proved right—washing your dirty hands does remove harmful bacteria.

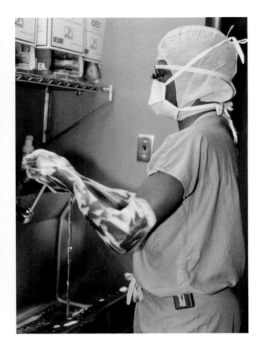

▲ A surgeon scrubs his arms and hands before an operation to remove germs that might infect his patient. Cleanliness in hospitals is seen as vital to prevent infection—just as Dr. Ignaz Semmelweis had suggested in the 1840s but was ignored.

▲ An illustration drawn in 1877 by pioneering microbe hunter Robert Koch showing the life history of the bacterium that causes the disease anthrax.

Bacteria killers

When the cause of infectious diseases was known, the fight against microbes began. In 1865 English surgeon Joseph Lister (1827–1912) used carbolic acid (phenol) spray to kill microorganisms during operations. At this time in the U.S. and Europe sewers were built to remove waste and to prevent the contamination of drinking water by harmful bacteria. Then the search for microbe-killing drugs began. Possibly the most significant discovery happened in 1928 when bacteriologist Alexander Fleming (1881–1955) found that a chemical (penicillin) released by a mold called *Penicillium* killed disease-causing bacteria. Full-scale production of penicillin began in the 1940s. Since then penicillin and other antibiotics (bacteria-killing drugs) have saved the lives of millions of people.

Microbes as partners

Microorganisms sometimes form partnerships with other living things in a close relationship called symbiosis ("living together"). Symbiotic relationships take different forms, including mutualism and parasitism. Mutualism is a relationship in which both partners benefit, and neither can survive without the other. Microbes in a mutual relationship help their larger partner, or host, in return for a safe place to live. Parasitism (see pages 48–49), on the other hand, only benefits one partner (the microbe) at the expense of another and often causes disease.

Wood eaters

Many animals feed on plants, and the chief part of their diet is the substance cellulose, the main component of a plant's supporting framework. However, most plant eaters cannot digest energy-rich cellulose. They can only gain benefits from this valuable food source through a partnership with cellulose-digesting microorganisms. Termites, for example, are insects that feed on wood and live in large colonies. The termites that search for food are called workers. Living inside each worker's stomach are many thousands of protists, especially *Trichonympha*. They digest the tiny cellulose-rich wood chips that the worker swallows and release the nutrients that allow the termite—and colony—to live.

abomasum

omasum

rumen

reticulum

◄ This LM shows the protist *Trichonympha*, 200μm long, using its many beating flagella to move inside a termite's stomach. Magnification: x500

▲ The digestive system of cattle includes a large stomach with four chambers (in order): rumen, reticulum, omasum, and abomasum.

◄ Worker termites enter and leave their nest as they search for wood and other plant food for the rest of the colony, including soldier termites—like the one in the center of the photo (large head and jaws). Magnification: x8.5

Chewing the cud

They may be much larger than termites, but cattle have similar digestive problems. They belong to a group of plant eaters called ruminants that also includes sheep and giraffes. A ruminant's stomach consists of four compartments including a large rumen (thus the name "ruminant") that provides a warm home for trillions of bacteria and protists. As a cow grazes, it eats cellulose-rich grass that is digested by microbes in the rumen. Part-digested food is then regurgitated back to the mouth as "cud," which is chewed again before returning to the rumen. Digestion is completed in the omasum and intestines, where some of the helpful and nutrient-rich microorganisms are also digested.

▶ This brown-throated three-toed sloth (*Bradypus variegatus*) appears greenish because of green cyanobacteria in its shaggy overcoat of coarse hair. In its tropical rain forest home the artificial green color provides the slow-moving sloth with camouflage, making it less visible to harpy eagles and other predators.

▲ This TEM shows one of the types of bacteria (red and green) that are found in the rumen of cows. Along with some protists, these bacteria work to break down plant material (gray and brown) that cannot be digested by the cow. Magnification: **x100,000**

Catching sunlight

Cyanobacteria and algae (protists) are photosynthetic microorganisms that make food using sunlight energy. Some form partnerships with animals. Giant clams are relatives of oysters that live in shallow tropical seas. Positioned vertically, clams open their shells to draw in a current of seawater that carries food particles. This also exposes their mantle, a fringe of soft tissue that contains masses of photosynthetic algae, called zooxanthellae, that provide the clam with a vital source of energy-rich sugars. Other marine animals, including corals, also contain zooxanthellae. A different relationship exists between slow-moving sloths and cyanobacteria. In the warm, wet conditions of a tropical rain forest green cyanobacteria thrive inside the long, grooved hairs of the sloth. The green coloration this gives the sloth enables it to merge with its leafy surroundings and protects it from predators.

◀ A view looking down into the gape (opening) between the two hinged valves (shells) of a giant clam (*Tridacna crocea*). The brightly colored soft tissue, or mantle, that overlaps the edges of the valves is home to symbiotic algae that provide food for the clam.

Persistent parasites

Parasites live in or on other organisms. As you have read, parasitic bacteria and viruses cause diseases, but so do other tiny organisms. Spread by insects, protists cause devastating diseases such as sleeping sickness and malaria, while roundworms cause elephantiasis. These are persistent parasites that easily deceive the body's immune system, so they are difficult to eliminate, even with the help of medicine. However, other protists, such as *Giardia*, can be treated successfully.

▼ Two *Plasmodium* parasites (blue and pink) can be seen in this TEM of a cross section through a red blood cell. *Plasmodium* causes malaria, growing and multiplying within red blood cells. Magnification: **x9,125**

Sleeping sickness

Across central Africa people are prey to a large biting fly—called the tsetse fly—that can spread a deadly protist when it feeds on human blood. That protist is *Trypanosoma brucei*, the cause of trypanosomiasis, or sleeping sickness. When the tsetse fly bites, the protist enters the bloodstream, multiplies, and eventually reaches the brain. At first it makes a person feel weak and tired (thus the name "sleeping sickness"), but eventually it leads to a coma and death. More than 300,000 people are affected, with another 25,000 infected every year.

▶ Wriggling among the mass of red blood cells in this SEM is the parasitic protist *Trypanosoma brucei* (yellow), which causes sleeping sickness. Magnification: **x5,000**

Sweats and fevers

Malaria occurs in most tropical and subtropical regions, including central Africa, South America, and Southeast Asia. It affects around 200 million people and kills around two million every year. The malarial parasite—a protist called *Plasmodium*—is carried from person to person by *Anopheles* mosquitoes. When an infected female mosquito pierces the skin to feed on blood, she injects *Plasmodium* into the bloodstream. The tiny parasites invade red blood cells, where they grow and multiply. The blood cells then burst, releasing a variety of parasites that invade more blood cells. This bursting causes the symptoms of malaria—severe chills, a burning fever of 104°F (40°C), and pouring sweats.

▶ A tsetse fly (*Glossina morsitans*) pierces human skin in order to feed on blood. Tsetse flies carry the parasitic protist that causes the disease sleeping sickness, releasing the parasite into the bloodstream as they feed. Magnification: **x8**

◀ A person's left leg and foot show the swelling and "elephantlike" skin thickening that is typical of the disease elephantiasis. It is caused by *Wuchereria bancrofti* roundworms that block the body's lymph vessels.

▲ This LM shows human blood containing a microfilaria (around 250µm long) of the roundworm that causes elephantiasis. **Magnification: x500**

Upset stomachs

Not all pathogenic protists are injected by insects into the bloodstream. *Giardia lamblia* infects the small intestine, producing foul-smelling diarrhea—a condition known as giardiasis. People pick up the parasite by drinking water or eating food that has been contaminated with *Giardia* cysts passed out in other people's or animals' feces. *Giardia* was first seen in 1681 by the microscopist Antoni van Leeuwenhoek. During a bad bout of diarrhea, he looked at a sample of his own feces under a microscope and found it to be swarming with the tiny pear-shaped creatures.

Worm threat

The tropical disease elephantiasis is also spread by mosquitoes but is caused by roundworms, not protists. It affects 100 million people in South America, central Africa, and Asia and causes severe swelling of the limbs. As it feeds, an infected mosquito injects tiny microfilariae (larvae) of the roundworm *Wuchereria bancrofti* into a person's bloodstream. The microfilariae enter lymphatic vessels, a network of tubes that drains fluid from the body's tissues back into the bloodstream. There they grow into larger adult worms that block the lymphatic vessels and then cause fluid to build up in the tissues, making them swell dramatically.

▶ This SEM shows protist parasite *Giardia lamblia* inside the small intestine (red). Around 10µm long, *Giardia* uses a sucking disk (darker green) to attach itself to the intestine wall. **Magnification: x2,100**

Life on humans

From birth our bodies are home to many different types of bacteria and fungi. These microorganisms occupy the body's outer surfaces (skin and eyes) and inner surfaces, including the nose, mouth, and the large intestine. A person normally carries around 1,000 trillion microorganisms—ten times the number of their own body cells. Most are permanent residents that harmlessly coexist with us—and even help us because they destroy pathogens that would cause diseases. The body is also home to mini animals, including harmless eyelash mites, and harmful opportunists such as lice and itch mites.

▲ This handprint is made up of colonies of skin microbes. A hand was pressed onto agar gel, leaving behind bacteria and fungi, which multiplied to form the colonies seen here.

Stomach dwellers

Warm and moist, our colon (the longest section of the large intestine) contains more bacteria than any other body part. These trillions of mostly harmless bacteria help us in various ways. Colon bacteria protect us from infections by producing chemicals that stop or kill pathogens. They make B vitamins and vitamin K, essential nutrients that are absorbed into our blood. They also digest food that our stomach cannot digest, a process that releases around 15 fl. oz. (500ml) of smelly gases daily. Around 30 percent of our feces is bacteria (more than 100 billion bacteria daily). This is why we should wash our hands after using the bathroom.

▲ This SEM shows the lining of the large intestine covered with rod-shaped *Escherichia coli* bacteria, each around 4μm long, one of the many types of bacteria in the human stomach. *E. coli* is usually harmless. Magnification: **x3,060**

▼ Three eyelash mites (*Demodex folliculorum*) protrude from their hair-follicle home in this SEM. Magnification: **x360**

On the surface

Each square inch of our skin is covered by between 10,000 and one million microbes, depending on how moist the skin is (the more moist, the better). But it is not easy for them to survive there. Salty sweat and germ-killing oily secretions kill many microorganisms. Those bacteria and fungi that do settle are usually harmless. More importantly, they form a community that stops harmful pathogens from living there and helps keep our skin healthy. As well as microbes, all of us unknowingly have a population of eyelash mites living on our bodies. These tiny spider relatives, sausage-shaped and only 0.25mm long, squeeze into the follicles (pits in the skin) from which eyelashes grow. There they live harmlessly on a diet of dead skin cells and oily secretions.

Hair grippers

Lice (singular—louse) are tiny wingless insects that pierce human skin, feed on blood, and make us itch. Head lice grip tightly to scalp hairs using their curved claws, making them very difficult to dislodge. Common among young children, head lice spread by scampering from one head to another. Female head lice lay daily batches of eggs—called nits—and attach them to hairs using a very strong "glue." Normal hair washing does not get rid of lice or nits. A special louse-killing shampoo has to be used, along with a fine-tooth comb in order to remove nits and dead lice.

Intense itching

The skin-dwelling scabies mite is also, for good reason, known as the itch mite. Using piercing mouthparts, the female mite digs into the skin, excavating tunnels up to 0.08 in. (2cm) long in which she lays eggs. New generations of mites hatch from the eggs within days. The combination of burrowing and mite feces seriously irritates the skin, resulting in a disease called scabies that causes intense itching, especially at night. Although mites pass easily from person to person, scabies infections are rare and can be treated with mite-killing lotions.

◀ The human head louse (*Pediculus humanus capitis*) in this SEM is around 3mm long and is clinging tightly, especially its head, to three strands of scalp hair using its six clawed legs. Magnification: **x80**

▼ This SEM shows a female scabies mite (*Sarcoptes scabiei*) that is around 0.5mm long on human skin. Backward-pointing spines prevent her from being dislodged from skin tunnels. Magnification: **x260**

Natural cycles

Living things are constructed from key elements such as carbon and nitrogen. There is only a finite supply of these substances, so for life to continue they must be returned or recycled to the environment when organisms die. Soil microorganisms and mini animals play a key role in recycling by rotting dead remains and releasing reusable substances into the environment. The continuous exchange of substances between the environment and organisms is called a cycle.

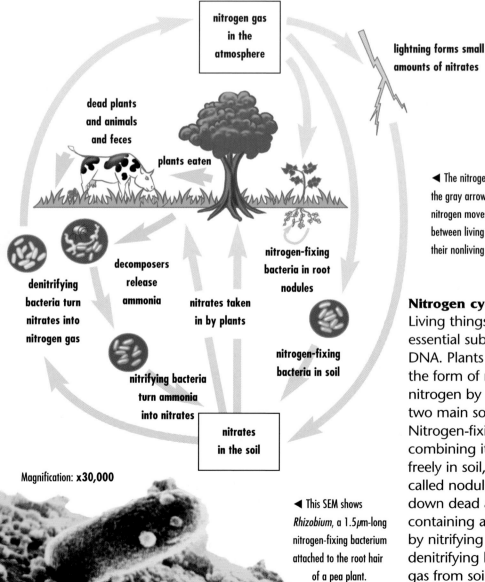

nitrogen gas
in the
atmosphere

lightning forms small
amounts of nitrates

dead plants
and animals
and feces

plants eaten

denitrifying
bacteria turn
nitrates into
nitrogen gas

decomposers
release
ammonia

nitrates taken
in by plants

nitrogen-fixing
bacteria in root
nodules

nitrifying bacteria
turn ammonia
into nitrates

nitrogen-fixing
bacteria in soil

nitrates
in the soil

Magnification: x30,000

◄ The nitrogen cycle—
the gray arrows show how
nitrogen moves continuously
between living organisms and
their nonliving surroundings.

◄ This SEM shows
Rhizobium, a 1.5µm-long
nitrogen-fixing bacterium
attached to the root hair
of a pea plant.

Nitrogen cycle

Living things use nitrogen to make essential substances such as proteins and DNA. Plants take in nitrogen from soil in the form of nitrates, and animals obtain their nitrogen by eating plants. Nitrates come from two main sources—nitrogen fixers and decomposers. Nitrogen-fixing bacteria "fix" nitrogen gas in the air, combining it with oxygen to make nitrates. Some exist freely in soil, while others live in plant root swellings called nodules. Decomposing fungi and bacteria break down dead animals and plants and release nitrogen-containing ammonia. This is converted into nitrates by nitrifying bacteria. The cycle is completed by denitrifying bacteria, which release nitrogen gas from soil nitrates back into the air.

carbon dioxide
in the
atmosphere

decomposers
release carbon
dioxide by
respiration

carbon dioxide
released by
respiration in
animals and
plants

carbon dioxide
taken up by
plants during
photosynthesis

dead animals
and plants

decomposers

▲ The carbon cycle—carbon
continually passes between
carbon dioxide in air and
carbon-containing substances
in living organisms.

◄ This 1mm-long springtail
is one of the tiny wingless
soil insects that feed on plant
remains. Magnification: **x190**

Carbon cycle

Carbon forms the "backbone" of the molecules
that build and run organisms. Their carbon comes,
directly or indirectly, from carbon dioxide in the air.
Plants take in carbon dioxide during photosynthesis,
using it to make energy-rich sugars and plant-building
substances. When animals eat plants, carbon-containing
substances are passed on. Both animals and plants get
energy from sugars through cell respiration, which releases
waste carbon dioxide into the air. When animals and plants
die, their remains rot as they are broken down by soil
decomposers, which respire and release carbon dioxide into
the air. Carbon dioxide release completes the carbon cycle.

Life in soil

As well as rock particles and dead matter, every
handful of soil contains hundreds of mini animals, millions of
microscopic fungi, and billions of bacteria. Known collectively
as decomposers, these tiny organisms break down plant and
animal remains, releasing vital elements, such as carbon
and nitrogen, back into the environment to be used again.
Nutrients, such as nitrates, that are released into the soil
by decomposers are taken in by plant roots, making soil
an ideal place for plant growth.

Magnification: **x200**

◄ This LM shows *Ceratium*, a 300μm-long dinoflagellate found in marine phytoplankton. *Ceratium* has long spines that help it float and flagella that move it toward sunlight.

Ocean life

O ceans cover 70 percent of Earth's surface. All living things in the oceans depend on plankton—the trillions of microorganisms that float close to the surface. Plankton includes both plantlike phytoplankton and zooplankton (protozoa and mini animals). The name plankton means "wandering"—many planktonic creatures can swim but are so tiny that they are swept along by ocean currents.

Phytoplankton

Phytoplankton contains chlorophyll and other pigments that "trap" sunlight and use it to make food by photosynthesis. Phytoplankton includes algae (plantlike protists), such as dinoflagellates, as well as cyanobacteria. Importantly, these organisms provide food for zooplankton and thus for all other ocean creatures. They also release oxygen into the air.

▲ This satellite photograph from NASA's SeaWiFS (Sea-Viewing Wide Field-of-View Sensor) Project uses colors to show the distribution of phytoplankton in the oceans. Red areas have the most phytoplankton, continuing through orange, yellow, green, and light blue, which has the least phytoplankton.

Uneven distribution

Phytoplankton is not spread evenly across the oceans but thrives where seawater contains high levels of nutrients such as nitrogen. These high levels occur in cold waters since currents bring nutrient-rich water from the depths where dead creatures decay and are recycled. They also occur where rivers wash nutrients into the sea. Amounts of phytoplankton are much lower in tropical oceans, where little mixing occurs between surface water and deeper water.

Zooplankton

Ocean zooplankton contains types of most sea creatures. Some, such as copepods, spend their lives floating in the plankton. Others, such as the larvae of jellyfish, echinoderms (sea urchins and starfish), crustaceans, and fish, live in the plankton when young but leave as they develop into adults. Zooplankton also contains protozoa, including radiolarians and foraminiferans, which have delicate skeletons made of, respectively, silica and calcium carbonate.

Magnification: x500

killer whale

porpoise

cod

herring

zooplankton

phytoplankton

► Plankton forms the first links in ocean food chains like this one. Arrows indicate what eats what—for example, herring eat zooplankton—and shows the direction in which energy and nutrients pass from one organism to another.

◄ The most abundant algae in marine phytoplankton, diatoms have outer cases made of silica. Each case has two parts that fit together like a box and its lid. As this LM shows, diatom cases have intricate patterns and a wide variety of shapes.

Ocean food chains

A food chain links up to six species in a particular habitat according to what they eat and what eats them. At its base is a producer—a plant or plantlike organism that uses sunlight to trap energy that passes to species higher up in the chain. Phytoplankton is the producer in oceans. In the example of an ocean food chain (above, right) phytoplankton is eaten by zooplankton that, in turn, are eaten by herring, cod, porpoises, and killer whales.

Ancient remains

When plankton die, any hard parts, such as the skeletons or shells, sink to the seabed. Over millions of years these tiny remains accumulate to form a thick layer that eventually turns into rocks. Calcium carbonate from foraminiferan shells forms limestone and chalk, exposed as white cliffs where land meets the sea. Glasslike silica shells from diatoms and other protists form the rock diatomite, which has many uses, including as a mild abrasive in toothpaste.

► Seen under a light microscope, this sample taken from the ocean's surface reveals some of the minute creatures that make up marine zooplankton. Easily visible here are circular, tentacled medusae—the larvae of jellyfish and their relatives. Darting between them using their long antennae are tiny crustaceans including copepods. Making up the mixture are the young of other types of animals.
Magnification: x30

Living in extremes

We feel uncomfortable if summer temperatures hit 95°F (35°C), but how would we cope if they reached 176°F (80°C)? Being that hot would certainly kill us and most other living things. So would being put in a freezer, exposed to radiation, covered in acid, baked by the desert sun, or being entombed in rocks. Yet there are certain bacteria that not only survive but actually thrive under such impossibly harsh conditions. Together, these resilient organisms are known as extremophiles ("lovers of extremes").

▲ The world's toughest bacterium, *Deinococcus radiodurans*, is not only unusually resistant to extreme heat, cold, and droughts but also to deadly radiation. This TEM shows *D. radiodurans* arranged as a tetrad (four linked cells), with each cell around 2.5μm across.
Magnification: **x15,600**

Extremophiles

In Yellowstone National Park (in Idaho, Montana, and Wyoming) the scalding hot springs that bubble up through Earth's crust seem too hot for any form of life. Yet thermophilic ("heat-loving") bacteria that can tolerate temperatures of 185°F (85°C) or more thrive here. Some even live in hot water that is acidic enough to dissolve metal. In the deep sea the thermophilic bacteria that live close to vents that pour super-heated water onto the seabed include record-breaking *Pyrolobus fumarii*, a survivor at an incredible 235°F (113°C). Halophilic ("salt-loving") microbes live in salt lakes, such as the Dead Sea, where nothing else can tolerate the saltiness. Cryophilic ("cold-loving") bacteria survive in Antarctica at temperatures as low as -76°F (-60°C). Other bacteria can exist in solid rocks that are 1.9 mi. (3km) below Earth's surface.

◄ Clouds of steam rise from the Grand Prismatic Spring in Yellowstone National Park. The rings of yellow and green are formed by different types of bacteria that thrive despite the high temperatures.

Radiation resistant

The most extreme of all extremophiles must be the bacterium *Deinococcus radiodurans*. Its name, meaning "strange berry that withstands radiation," reveals its unusual ability. Radiation consists of high-energy alpha, beta, and gamma rays, given off by radioactive substances, that can damage living things. *D. radiodurans* can survive exposure to more than 3,000 times the radiation it would take to kill a person. It is also resistant to extreme heat, bitter cold, cell-damaging chemicals, and dehydration. Research is under way to see if this supermicrobe can be used to convert lethal radioactive waste into something less harmful.

Suspended animation

Most bacteria are not extremophiles, but many survive tough times by going into suspended animation. They form apparently lifeless spores, called endospores, each surrounded by a thick wall that can resist extremes of heat, cold, acidity, or toxic chemicals. Endospores can last for days, decades, or millions of years. If conditions become hospitable, the endospore splits open, and the bacterium returns to life. Mini animals called tardigrades use a similar strategy. Wet-loving tardigrades survive dry periods by pulling in their eight stumpy legs, drying out, shutting down their metabolism, and secreting a protective coat around their shrunken bodies. They can stay in this state for years, swelling up and returning to life once wet conditions return.

Magnification: **x300**

▲ This SEM shows *Macrobiotus richtersii*, a 300µm-long tardigrade. Also called water bears, these mini animals live in damp and wet places but can go into suspended animation if their habitat dries up.

Space survivors?

In space it is bitterly cold, with no air or oxygen, and there is constant exposure to lethal gamma and other cosmic rays. But astrobiologists (scientists who search for life on other planets) reason that if life can survive harsh conditions on Earth, then why not in space? Some argue that meteorites or comets could carry bacterial endospores—or that *D. radiodurans* evolved on Mars and then traveled to Earth through space. Or even that life first arrived on Earth billions of years ago on microbe-laden rocks from other planets. Science fiction or science fact? One day we might discover the answer.

▶ In space conditions are unbelievably tough. But some scientists have suggested that bacteria could survive there and that they may have even arrived on Earth from other planets.

SUMMARY OF CHAPTER 3: INSIDE THE MICROWORLD

Enemies or allies?

Are microorganisms our enemies or allies? They certainly affect us by causing killer diseases, such as plague, AIDS, and malaria, and a range of less serious ailments—from colds to athlete's foot. But science has revealed not only which microbe causes which disease but also how the body defends itself and how we can protect ourselves using vaccinations and antibiotics. The seriousness of disease overshadows the fact that only a few microbes are harmful. Most are harmless, and some are allies, for example by helping us make food and medicine.

Microbes in nature

Microorganisms also benefit all living things by playing key roles in the

A penicillin pellet (white) has a clear zone around it (black) showing where bacteria (green) have been killed by the antibiotic.

cycles of nature. When organisms die, for example, microbes recycle their remains, replenishing the finite supply of nutrients that living things need in order to survive. In the oceans tiny plantlike plankton that trap sunlight energy are the food source for all marine life, at the same time releasing oxygen for us and other creatures to breathe in. Throughout nature microbes form beneficial alliances with other organisms so that both have an improved chance of survival. However, some relationships benefit one partner and harm the other such as the parasitic protists and worms that infect humans and other animals.

Survive and thrive

We know that microorganisms greatly outnumber us, have existed on Earth long before humans—possibly arriving as Earth's first inhabitants from space—and will continue to exist long after we have become extinct. Some even survive and thrive under extreme conditions of cold, heat, and radiation that would kill the rest of us. As Louis Pasteur famously said when he acknowledged their superiority, "It is microbes that will have the last word."

Go further . . .

Learn a lot more about microbiology and microbiologists at: www.microbeworld.org/ htm/aboutmicro/abt_start.htm

See a cartoon of the discovery of the polio vaccine at: www.pbs.org/ wgbh/aso/ontheedge/polio/

For information about possible microbes in space go to: http://quest.arc.nasa.gov/projects/ astrobiology/fieldwork/students.html

Read more about the *D. radiodurans*: http://science.nasa.gov/newhome/ headlines/ast14dec99_1.htm

Microscopic Monsters by Nick Arnold (Scholastic, 2001)

Astrobiologist
Studies the possibility of life existing in space.

Biotechnologist
Studies the use of microorganisms in areas such as medicine and food.

Environmental microbiologist
Investigates the use of microbes to remove pollutants from the environment.

Epidemiologist
Studies diseases and how they are transmitted through populations.

Immunologist
Studies the body's immune system and the use of vaccines to control infections.

See where penicillin was discovered: Alexander Fleming Laboratory Museum
St. Mary's Hospital
Praed Street
London W2 1NY
England
Phone: +44 (0) 20 7886 6528
www.st-marys.nhs.uk/ about/fleming_museum.htm

Visit the MicroZoo at:
Armand-Frappier Museum
531 Boulevard des Prairies
Laval (Québec)
Canada H7V 1B7
Phone: (450) 686-5641
www.musee-afrappier.qc.ca/ anglais/MicroZoo.htm

Glossary

absorbed
Describes something taken in by an organism from its surroundings.

acid
A watery liquid that can dissolve metals, chalk, and tooth enamel.

agar
A gel made from seaweed, used as part of a medium for growing bacteria and fungi.

algae
Plantlike protists such as diatoms.

anthrax
A bacterial disease of cattle and humans that affects the skin and lungs.

antibiotic
A drug used to treat bacterial infections.

billion
A number equal to one thousand million (1,000,000,000).

budding
The way in which some microscopic organisms reproduce by growing a bud that forms a new full-size organism.

calcium carbonate (chalk)
A solid white substance that forms the shells or cases of certain protists.

carbolic acid
A liquid used in the 1800s as the first antiseptic to prevent the infection of wounds.

carbon dioxide
The gas released into the air by organisms as a waste product of cell respiration.

cell
A tiny living unit from which organisms are made.

cell respiration
The process by which cells release energy from sugars.

cellulose
The substance from which plant cell walls are constructed.

chemical
A general name for substances that make up both living and nonliving things.

cilia (singular—cilium)
Short, hairlike structures on the outside of certain microbes that produce movement.

conquistadores
Soldiers from Spain who occupied parts of Central and South America in the 1500s.

contamination
The addition of a harmful microorganism or substance to food or water.

convex
Describes a lens with two surfaces that curve outward.

crustaceans
A group of animals with hard outer skeletons and jointed limbs that includes water fleas, crabs, and lobsters.

decomposers
Organisms, mostly microbes, that feed on dead matter and break it down.

decomposition
The process by which dead matter is broken down into simple substances.

SEM of pseudoscorpion
Magnification: x48

disease
A failure in one or more of the body's systems caused, in the case of an infectious disease, by a pathogen.

DNA (deoxyribonucleic acid)
The chemical found in all cells that carries the instructions needed to build an organism.

electron
One of a number of tiny particles found inside atoms, the building blocks of all matter.

electron microscope
A microscope that uses a beam of electrons, instead of light, to produce an image.

enamel
The hard white layer that covers a tooth.

energy
The capacity of an organism to do work, for example to move.

epidemic
An outbreak of infectious disease that affects many people at the same time.

feces
The solid waste that passes out of an animal.

TEM of a *Streptococcus* bacterium
Magnification: x85,000

flagella (singular—flagellum)
The long, hairlike projections on some bacteria and protists that cause movement.

flu (influenza)
A viral disease that causes fever and aching joints.

fruiting body
A structure produced by fungi that makes, stores, and releases spores.

germinate
To grow from a spore released by a fungus.

hyphae (singular—hypha)
The microscopic, threadlike filaments that make up most fungi and through which fungi feed.

immune system
The system in the body that protects the body from infections.

immunity
The ability of the body's immune system to protect it against specific diseases.

infect
In the case of a pathogen, to invade and multiply in or on another organism.

infection
The multiplication of pathogens in or on an organism.

intestines
The tubes in an animal's digestive system in which food is digested and absorbed.

leaf litter
A layer of dead plant matter on the soil.

LM (light micrograph)
A photograph taken using a light microscope.

membrane
A thin layer that surrounds a cell.

metabolism
All the chemical processes that take place inside a living organism that keep it alive.

microbe
A general name given to a microorganism.

microbiology
The study of microorganisms.

micrograph
A photograph of a minute organism or object as seen though a microscope.

SEM of a foraminiferan shell
Magnification: x375

mildew
A type of fungus that infects plants.

mold
A type of microscopic fungus that commonly grows on and spoils food.

mucus
A thick, slimy, and protective liquid produced in the nose and throat.

multicellular
Describes an organism made up
of many cells.

nitrogen
A gas found in the air.

nutrients
Substances needed by an organism to provide
energy and for normal growth and repair.

organism
Any living thing.

oxygen
A gas in the air that is used by organisms
to release energy during cell respiration.

parasite
An organism that lives on or in—and feeds
on—another organism.

pathogen
A microbe that causes disease. Also called
a germ.

phagocyte
A general name for a white blood cell that
engulfs and digests pathogenic microbes.

photosynthesis
The process in plants, algae, and
cyanobacteria that uses sunlight energy to
make food from carbon dioxide and water.

pigment
A substance that gives an organism
its color.

plankton
The mass of microscopic organisms that
drift on the surface waters of seas and lakes.

protein
One of a group of substances that
perform many roles in all organisms,
including construction.

radiation
High-energy rays or particles that
can damage living organisms.

reproduce
To multiply, or produce offspring.

RNA (ribonucleic acid)
The chemical found in certain viruses
that carries instructions needed to
build new viruses.

SEM (scanning electron micrograph)
A photograph taken using a scanning
electron microscope.

silica
A glasslike substance that forms the
shells of certain protists and is also
found in sand.

spontaneous
Describes something that happens
suddenly without any obvious cause.

SEM of a marine copepod Magnification: **x14**

spores
Minute packages of cells that enable fungi
to reproduce and spread.

stagnant
Describes water that is still, contains
rotting matter, and smells bad.

strain
A special type of a particular species
of organism.

TEM (transmission electron micrograph)
A photograph taken using a transmission
electron microscope.

toxin
A substance produced by certain
pathogens that damages the
organism that it infects.

trillion
A number equal to one million million
(1,000,000,000,000).

tropical
Relating to hot regions close to the equator.

unicellular
Describes an organism made up of one cell.

vaccination
An injection of a killed or weakened pathogen
or toxin to give protection against a disease.

vegetable protein
Food manufactured from a protein-rich
plant source such as soybeans.

Index

Acknowledgments

The publisher would like to thank the following for permission to reproduce their material. Every care has been taken to trace copyright holders. However, if there have been unintentional omissions or failure to trace copyright holders, we apologize and will, if informed, endeavor to make corrections in any future edition.

Key: *b* = bottom, *c* = center, *l* = left, *r* = right, *t* = top

Cover Volker Steger/Christian Bardele/Science Photo Library (SPL); 2–3 Lepus/SPL; 4–5*b* Eye of Science/SPL; 7*t* Lepus/SPL; 8*bl* R. Maisonneuve, Publiphoto Diffusion/SPL; 8–9*tc* Dr. Gary Gaugler/SPL; 8–9*c* Sinclair Stammers/SPL; 9*tr* Biophoto Associates/SPL; 9*br* Andrew Syred/SPL; 10*cl* BSIP, Cavallini James/SPL; 10*c* Dr. Gary Gaugler/SPL; 10*cr* SPL; 11*tr* K. H. Kjeldsen/SPL; 11*cl* Biophoto Associates/SPL; 11*c* © Dennis Kunkel Microscopy, Inc.; 11*cr* Robert Harding; 12*bl* Dr. Jeremy Burgess/SPL; 13*cr* Michael Abbey; 14*bl* Dr. Linda Stannard, UCT/SPL; 14–15*tc* Manfred Kage/Oxford Scientific Films (OSF); 14*br* A. B. Dowsett/SPL; 15*tr* © Dennis Kunkel Microscopy, Inc.; 15*br* Pascal Goetgheluck/SPL; 16*bl* Steve Hopkin/ardea.com; 17*tr* John Reader/SPL; 18*bl* Eric Grave/SPL; 19*cr* Eric Grave/SPL; 19*tr* Sinclair Stammers/SPL; 19*br* Francis Leroy, Biocosmos/SPL; 20*tl* Andrew Syred/SPL; 21*b* © Dennis Kunkel Microscopy, Inc.; 22*bl* Andrew Syred/SPL; 22*tl* BSIP, Cavallini James/SPL; 22*tr* Victor Habbick Visions/SPL; 22–23 *Background* Biozentrum, University of Basel/SPL; 25*br* Cristina Pedrazzini/SPL; 24*bl* © Dennis Kunkel Microscopy, Inc.; 25 *E .coli sequence of growth* Eye of Science/SPL; 26*tl* D. Phillips/SPL; 26–27*c* Biophoto Associates/SPL; 27*tr* © Dennis Kunkel Microscopy, Inc.; 27*br* Dr. David Patterson/SPL; 28*bl* London Scientific Films/OSF; 28–29*c* Richard Packwood/OSF; 29*tr* Larry Michael/naturepl.com; 29*cl* Microfield Scientific Ltd./SPL; 30*tl* David M. Dennis/OSF; 30*bl* www.Micrographia.com; 30–31*b* © Dennis Kunkel Microscopy, Inc.; 31*tr* Kim Taylor/Bruce Coleman Collection; 31*br* Manfred Kage/Still Pictures; 32*tl* Dr. Immo Rantala/SPL; 33*b* Andrew McClenaghan/SPL; 34*tl* Dr. Jeremy Burgess/SPL; 34*bl* Lowell Georgia/SPL; 34*cl* Alfred Pasieka/SPL; 34–35*bc* Philippe Psaila/SPL; 35*tr* Richard T. Nowitz/Corbis; 35*cr* Russell Kightley/SPL; 35*br* NIBSC/SPL; 36*cl* David Scharf/SPL; 36*bl* Dr. Tony Brain/SPL; 36–37*c* Bettmann/Corbis; 37*tr* © Dennis Kunkel Microscopy, Inc.; 37*br* Owen Franken/Corbis; 38*tl* Sami Sarkis/Alamy; 38*bl* Rex Features; 38*br* Biophoto Associates/SPL; 39*tl* Brian Hawkes/NHPA; 39*r* Holt Studios/Nigel Cattlin; 40*bl* Linda Steinmark, Custom medical stock photo, SPL; 40*br* Dr. Steve Patterson/SPL; 40–41 Dr. Tony Brain/SPL; 40*tr* A. B. Dowsett/SPL; 41*tc* Sinclair Stammers/SPL; 41*tr* SPL; 42*c* BSIP, Cavallini James/SPL; 42*bl* Bernard Pierre Wolff/SPL; 42–43*tc* The Art Archive; 43*br* Bettman/Corbis; 44*tl* Archives Charmat/Bridgeman Art Library; 44–45*bc* Corbis; 43*tl* Richard T. Nowitz/SPL; 45*tr* Wellcome Library, London; 46*bl* OSF; 50*bl* (*background*) Eric Grave/SPL; 46*c* Richard T. Nowitz/Corbis; 46–47*tc* Dr. Kari Lounatmaa/SPL; 47*tr* Michael Fogden/OSF; 47*b* Georgette Douwma/SPL; 48*cl* CNRI/SPL; 48*br* Martin Dohrn/SPL; 48–49*t* SPL; 49*tr* Sinclair Stammers/SPL; 49*cl* R. Umesh Chandrian, TDR, WHO/SPL; 49*br* Lepus/SPL; 50*tl* Science Pictures Ltd./SPL; 50*bl* Eye of Science/SPL; 50*cr* SPL; 50*l* Garry Hunter for LAB/The Wellcome Trust; 50*br* Eye of Science/SPL; 52*bl* Dr. Jeremy Burgess/SPL; 52–53*c* Dr. Jeremy Burgess/SPL; 54*tl* Sinclair Stammers/SPL; 54*bl* provided by the SeaWiFS Project, NASA/Goddard Space Flight Center and ORBIMAGE; 54–55*tc* M. I. Walker/Wellcome Photo Library; 55*br* Douglas P. Wilson, Frank Lane Picture Agency/Corbis; 56*tl* Uniformed Services University of the Health Sciences, Bethesda, MD; 56*bl* Jim Brandenberg/Minden/FLPA; 57*tr* Microfield Scientific Ltd./SPL; 57*br* Dr. Fred Espenak/SPL; 58*cl* John Durham/SPL; 59*br* © Dennis Kunkel Microscopy, Inc.; 60*bl* Dr. Immo Rantala/SPL; 60–61*c* © Dennis Kunkel Microscopy, Inc.; 61*tr* © Dennis Kunkel Microscopy, Inc.; 64*br* © Dennis Kunkel Microscopy, Inc.

The publisher would like to thank the following illustrators:
Peter Clayman 50*c;* Sebastien Quigley (Linden Artists) 12–13, 16–17, 18*tl,* 18–19*c,* 22*bl,* 24–25, 27*cr,* 46*l,* 47*tr;*
Steve Weston (Linden Artists) 49*r.*

The author would like to thank Carron Brown for her diligence and enthusiasm, Peter Clayman for his inspired designs, the other members of the Kingfisher team for their hard work, and Dr. John Grainger for his pertinent comments.

SEM of a dust mite
Magnification: **x553**